AQA Mathematics

Teacher's Book

Unit 1 Higher

New GCSE

Series Editor
Paul Metcalf

Series Advisor
Andy Darbourne

Lead Authors
Sandra Burns
Shaun Procter-Green
Margaret Thornton

Authors
Tony Fisher
June Haighton
Anne Haworth
Gill Hewlett
Andrew Manning
Ginette McManus
Howard Prior
David Pritchard
Dave Ridgway
Paul Winters

Nelson Thornes

Published in 2010 by:
Nelson Thornes Ltd
Delta Place
27 Bath Road
CHELTENHAM
GL53 7TH
United Kingdom

10 11 12 13 14 / 10 9 8 7 6 5 4 3 2 1

A catalogue record for this book is available from the British Library

ISBN 978 1 4085 0624 0

Cover photograph: iStockphoto
Page make-up by Fakenham Photosetting, Norfolk

Printed in Croatia by Zrinski

Contents

Nelson Thornes and AQA

Nelson Thornes has worked in partnership with AQA to ensure that this book and the accompanying online resources offer you the best support for your teaching of the GCSE course.

All AQA endorsed resources undergo a thorough quality assurance process to ensure that their contents closely match the AQA specification. You can be confident that the content of materials branded with AQA's 'Exclusively Endorsed' logo have been written, checked and approved by AQA senior examiners, in order to achieve AQA's exclusive endorsement.

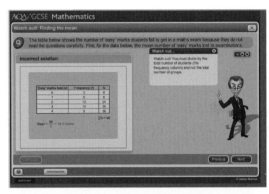

The print and online resources together unlock blended learning; this means that the links between the activities in the book and the activities online blend together to maximise students' understanding of a topic and help them achieve their potential.

These online resources are available on 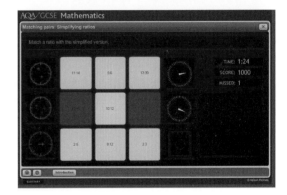 *kerboodle!* which can be accessed via the internet at **www.kerboodle.com/live**, anytime, anywhere.

If your school or college subscribes to *kerboodle!* you will be provided with your own personal login details. Once logged in, access your course and locate the required activity.

For more information and help on how to use *kerboodle!* visit **www.kerboodle.com**.

How to use this book

To help you unlock blended learning, we have referenced the activities in this book that have additional online coverage in *kerboodle!* by using this icon

The icons in this book show you the online resources available from the start of the new specification and will always be relevant.

In addition, to keep the blend up-to-date and engaging, we review customer feedback and may add new content onto *kerboodle!* after publication.

In the AQA Mathematics GCSE assessments (from first teaching 2010), students will be tested on the Assessment Objectives (AOs) below.

AO1 recall and use your knowledge of the prescribed content

AO2 select and apply mathematical methods in a range of contexts

AO3 interpret and analyse problems and generate strategies to solve them.

In order to fully enhance your teaching of these new assessments, Nelson Thornes has produced this book to offer teaching ideas, lesson help and examiner guidance to support the New AQA GCSE Mathematics Student Book. You will also find a wealth of electronic resources on our *kerboodle!* website **www.kerboodle.com**.

In each chapter of this Teacher Book, you will find the following:

Objectives provide AQA Specification references, with suggested grade boundaries, that will be covered in each Learn section within the Student Book.

kerboodle! resources

These show all the electronic resources on *kerboodle!* that are available to support the chapter.

 denotes where there are corresponding electronic resources on *kerboodle!*

You will see this icon throughout the Student Books, Teacher's Books and Revision Guides.

Starter activities

There is at least one Starter activity per Student Book Learn section. You can use them all or pick whichever suits your class best.

Plenary activities

Like the starter activities, these are activities from which you can choose as many as you like.

For each topic in the corresponding Student Book you will find:

 Learn...

This is identical to the Learn section that students will see in their books, plus additional examples or methods that may help support their understanding of the topic.

Teacher notes

These offer suggestions and guidance about ways in which you could expand your teaching by discussing particular points with your students.

Common errors

These highlight mistakes that are often made so you can help your students avoid them.

AQA Examiner's tip

These are suggestions from AQA examiners to help guide your students in preparing for their assessments, focusing on points to remember or consider carefully.

Bump up your grade

These are suggestions from AQA examiners on how to help your students achieve a higher grade, particularly targeted at students aiming for that all-important Grade C.

Consolidation chapters

Consolidation chapters are usually found at the end of each Student Book and contain questions on the content across the entire book. These chapters allow students to practise more AO2 and AO3 type questions, without any hints on the maths that they must use. These chapters will prepare your students for assessments where they will be required to find their own ways of answering questions. You can refer your students to these questions throughout the course so that they have plenty of practice for the exams. Electronic resources to support the consolidation chapter can be found on *kerboodle!* These include student worksheets, WebQuests and On Your Marks ... activities. Please see the Scheme of Work for more information.

 Fractions and decimals

Objectives

1.1 One quantity as a fraction of another	Specification	
D • find one quantity as a fraction of another	Calculate with fractions.	N2.7

1.2 Calculating with fractions	Specification	
D • solve problems involving fractions	Calculate with fractions.	N2.7
C • multiply and divide fractions • add and subtract mixed numbers		

1.3 Rounding	Specification	
C • round numbers to significant figures	Approximate to specified or appropriate degrees of accuracy including a given number of decimal places and significant figures.	N1.4

1.4 Upper and lower bounds	Specification	
B • find upper and lower bounds	Calculate and use upper and lower bounds.	N1.13h
A • use upper and lower bounds in calculations		

1.5 Calculating with bounds	Specification	
A • use upper and lower bounds in calculations	Calculate and use upper and lower bounds.	N1.13h

kerboodle! resources

- **k!** 0–9: Fraction calculations
- **k!** Interactive activity: Rounding
- **k!** 10 quick questions: Rounding
- **k!** Watch out!: Upper and lower bounds
- **k!** Worksheet: Fractions and decimals 1
- **k!** Worksheet: Fractions and decimals 2
- **k!** Test yourself: Rounding
- **k!** On your marks...: Fractions

Starter activities

Learn 1.1 1 Ask questions such as:
What fraction of this class are female?/wear glasses?/support Manchester United?
Discuss how you can work out the fractions, what makes it easy or difficult, why we would want to do this.

Learn 1.1 2 Give students some time to discuss, and find out, how to put fractions into their calculators, using the ▣ or a_c^b keys.

Learn 1.1 3 In this calculator unit, students have to become competent with the calculator functions on their calculators. Give them some practice by asking them to use their calculators to simplify fractions such as $\frac{155}{180}, \frac{35}{200}, \frac{623}{800}, \frac{165}{190}, \frac{740}{540}$.

Learn 1.2 4 Ask students to show on their mini-whiteboards:
- a mixed number
- an improper fraction
- a fraction equivalent to, for example, $\frac{3}{4}$

- a decimal fraction
- a unit fraction (a fraction with 1 as the numerator and any integer as the denominator)
- a pair of equivalent fractions
- a proper fraction
- the fraction $\frac{18}{54}$ in its lowest terms/simplest form
- the fraction $\frac{20}{3}$ as a mixed number.

Look out for errors and misconceptions. Encourage students to explore ideas and to use the correct vocabulary in their explanations.

Learn 1.2

5 Ask students to decide which is the bigger fraction in each pair below and explain their reasoning.

$$\frac{2}{3}, \frac{1}{3} \qquad \frac{2}{5}, \frac{4}{5} \qquad \frac{2}{7}, 1 \qquad \frac{4}{9}, \frac{4}{5} \qquad \frac{5}{8}, \frac{5}{3} \qquad \frac{9}{7}, 1 \qquad \frac{1}{2}, \frac{7}{16} \qquad \frac{2}{3}, \frac{3}{4}$$

As an extension, ask for a fraction in between each of the pairs.

Learn 1.3

6 Find some current numbers for attendance at gigs, football matches, and so on. Alternatively, use the following figures on average attendances of football clubs.

Club	Average attendance
Manchester United	75 304
Real Madrid C.F	74 895
FC Barcelona	73 913
Arsenal	60 040
Newcastle United	48 750
Liverpool F.C.	43 611
Chelsea	41 588
Tottenham Hotspur	35 929
Southampton	17 849

Ask students to give the numbers to the nearest thousand. Check results, address misconceptions and discuss why numbers are rounded for different purposes.

Learn 1.3

7 Give students a set of numbers such as 8.345, 8.4, 8.37, 8.3, 8.3127 and ask them to arrange these in order. Then ask them to find a number between each pair in the list.

This will give students an opportunity to practise working with decimals and you the opportunity to address anything they may find difficult.

Learn 1.4

8 Ask students to discuss what a statement such as 'There were 2500 people at the match' really means – were there exactly 2500 people? How many could there have been at the match? To get them thinking about the issues in this Learn section, you could extend this by discussing some of the following topics: A label on a bag of crisps says it weighs 30 g. Do you think this is accurate? Anna is asked how much money she has in the bank. She says about £500. How much do you think she might have? Aidan says he is 15 years old. What are the greatest and least ages Aidan could be?

Learn 1.4

9 Ask the students to think about and discuss in pairs what a diagram such as the one below means.

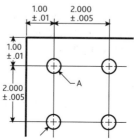

Answer: It is a diagram of an engineering component to be manufactured, indicating the limits within which the measurements must lie. The numbers are measurements in centimetres. Students may need to be told that the sign ± means plus or minus.

Plenary activities

Some of the above 'starter' activities could of course equally well be used as whole-class activities at the end of a lesson.

Learn 1.1

1 If you used the first starter, return to some of the questions asked at the beginning of the lesson to see whether students' understanding has developed and whether they are getting familiar with the process of working out one quantity as a fraction of another.

Learn 1.1

2 Ask students to work out, for example, 18 as a fraction of 30 and 30 as a fraction of 18 and other similar examples. Ask them what they notice and to explain why.

Students should notice that the second fraction is always the 'upside down' version of the first, though this may be hidden depending on the calculator mode employed. You can discuss changing from improper fractions to mixed numbers and vice versa. You may also wish to introduce, or remind the students of, the word 'reciprocal', which they will need later.

This is an opportunity for students to spot, and explain the reason for, a simple generalisation.

Learn 1.2

3 Play Fraction Bingo. Students draw a three-by-two grid and choose one of the nine fractions to write in each box.

$\frac{1}{3}, \frac{2}{3}, \frac{1}{4}, \frac{1}{2}, \frac{3}{4}, \frac{1}{5}, \frac{2}{5}, \frac{3}{5}, \frac{4}{5}$

Read out questions such as those below and tell students to cross off the answers on their grids. The first student to cross off all his/her numbers wins. Remind them that they can use their calculators.

$\frac{1}{3} + \frac{1}{6}$; half of a half; one-third of 2; $\frac{15}{25}$ in its simplest form; $\frac{1}{18} + \frac{1}{9} + \frac{1}{6}$; $2 \times \frac{3}{8}$;

20 as a fraction of 100; 0.8 as a fraction; one third of $1\frac{1}{5}$

An alternative to this is Mixed Fraction Bingo. Give students a set of mixed numbers and then give them improper fractions. Students cross off the grid if they have the matching mixed number.

Learn 1.2

4 Put a set of fractions such as $\frac{1}{2}, \frac{1}{3}, \frac{3}{5}, \frac{11}{20}$ on the board. Ask students, using calculators to help them, to find:

- which two fractions have the biggest total
- which two have the smallest total
- which two have a product closest to $\frac{1}{2}$
- which two fractions have the smallest difference

Discuss the methods students used to answer the questions.

Learn 1.2

5 Make a set of cards consisting of five fractions such as $1\frac{1}{2}, 3\frac{3}{4}, \frac{5}{9}, \frac{7}{8}$, five integers such as 25, 68, 33, 18, 54, and the operation symbols +, −, ×, ÷.

Choose a student who selects two numbers (fractions or integers) and an operation symbol and set them out as a calculation. The first student to use his/her calculator to get the correct answer gets a point.

Learn 1.2

6 Return to Starter 5 and ask students to describe, for someone else to use, how to find which of a pair of fractions is bigger. Discuss results and agree on a good description.

Learn 1.3

7 Ask students to list examples of measurements or statistics that they have seen in the media or use in everyday life or in other subjects.

For example,

- 7.7 million viewers tuned in on Saturday night.
- The government spent £135.7bn last year.
- Government to cut £2bn from schools' budget.

For each one, write down what they think is its accuracy. Discuss results, talk about the range of possible values a measurement can have. Ages and money provide interesting discussion points. This is good preparation for the next section.

Learn 1.3

8 Ask students: How many numbers are there between 12.9 and 13? Encourage discussion, argument, examples and agreement.

Learn 1.4

9 Discuss with the students where they have met tolerances in other areas of the curriculum or elsewhere to help them to see the relevance of the work they have done. For example, students of GCSE Design and Technology will be familiar with manufacturing within tolerances; in electronics resistors have a tolerance code. The idea has been used in AQA GSCE Statistics questions; in mathematics examinations students' answers sometimes have to be within certain tolerances, and so on.

Learn 1.5

10 Ask students to look at the four expressions below, involving four rounded numbers a, b, c and d and say, with reasons, which will give the biggest answer and which will give the smallest.

$$\frac{\text{max of } a - \text{max of } b}{\text{max of } c - \text{max of } d}$$

$$\frac{\text{max of } a - \text{min of } b}{\text{min of } c - \text{max of } d}$$

$$\frac{\text{max of } a - \text{min of } b}{\text{max of } c - \text{min of } d}$$

$$\frac{\text{min of } a - \text{max of } b}{\text{max of } c - \text{min of } d}$$

Teacher notes

Many students find fractions quite hard to do and real life does not provide much motivation (though the 'Did you know?' piece at the start of the Student Book chapter may provide some ideas); apart from simple halves and quarters, fractions other than percentages are little used currently, though they are a little more common in the USA where imperial units are still in use.

Working with decimals on a calculator should provide success and motivation and it gives a good opportunity to discuss, explore and practise efficient use of calculators and the intelligent interpretation of the calculator display.

Learn... 1.1 One quantity as a fraction of another

To work out one quantity as a fraction of another, write the first quantity as the **numerator** and the second as the **denominator**, then simplify the fraction.

To work out 35 as a fraction of 50, write 35 out of 50 as a fraction, $\frac{35}{50}$, then simplify to $\frac{7}{10}$
$\frac{35}{100}$ and $\frac{7}{10}$ are **equivalent fractions**. So, 35 is seven-tenths of 50.

Example: A swimmer has a target of 60 lengths of the pool to swim. He has done 45 lengths. What fraction of his target is this?

Solution: The fraction is 45 out of 60 $= \frac{45}{60} = \frac{3}{4}$ (The simplification can be done using the calculator, as students can practise in Starter 3, using the 🔲 or a^b_c keys.)

To get a denominator of 100 (to convert to a percentage) multiply by $\frac{25}{25}$

$$\frac{3}{4} = \frac{3 \times 25}{4 \times 25}$$

$$= \frac{75}{100}$$

$$= 75\%$$

Example: Dan's height was 1.64 m at the start of Year 11 and 1.68 m at the end of Year 11. By what fraction did Dan's height increase during Year 11?

Solution: Increase in Dan's height is 1.68 m − 1.64 m = 168 cm − 164 cm = 4 cm

Fraction increase in height $= \frac{4}{164}$

It is important to find the fraction of the original amount, in this case Dan's height at the start of the year, and that the units are the same.

Simplify this using the calculator: [🖩] 4 ▶ 164 $= \frac{1}{41}$

So Dan's height has increased by the fraction $\frac{1}{41}$

Teacher notes

This part of the mathematics curriculum is one of the most useful in everyday and work life but most adults are unable to calculate one number as a fraction or percentage of another. If students do not understand what they are doing, they tend to try to remember a rule that they often apply incorrectly, never being sure what goes on top of what. They need time to explore the situations and the opportunity to check that answers make sense, by working with some simple situations such as the fraction of males and females in the class; if there are 30 students in the class and 18 of them are female, the fraction is 18 out of 30, or $\frac{18}{30}$. Just to write one number on top of one another to get the fraction correct is the important first step. It may indeed be the only step, but usually the fraction needs to be simplified and, perhaps, to be converted into a decimal or percentage. The calculator should be used to simplify the resulting fraction, using the [🖩] or [a_c^b] keys depending on the calculators that your students are using. Make sure that they know how to work with the calculator they will be using in the exam.

Another important point is to convert units so that the numerator and the denominator are compatible. So, when working out 75 pence as a fraction of £3, both quantities have to be expressed in pence or both in pounds. You may wish to encourage students to try both and see which they find easier. Usually it is easier to work with whole numbers in a fraction, so in the case of money, using pence is probably the better option.

✗ Common errors

✗ Students who do not understand the process of expressing one quantity as a fraction of another may forget which number goes on top of the other.

✗ Not making sure the units match in the numerator and the denominator.

AQA/Examiner's tip

Working out one quantity as a fraction of another is often badly done in exams. It is helpful if the fraction is explicitly written down before any simplification or conversion is attempted.

Learn... 1.2 Calculating with fractions

In this unit you will be using a calculator to work with fractions. There is more work on fraction calculations in Unit 2.

With a calculator, you can use the fraction button [🖩] or [a_c^b] to do all fraction calculations.

For example, to do the calculation $\frac{3}{4} + \frac{2}{5}$, do this:

[🖩] 3 ▶ 4 ▶ [+] [🖩] 2 ▶ 5 [=]

or 3 [a_c^b] 4 [+] 2 [a_c^b] 5 [=]

which gives the answer $\frac{23}{20}$ or $1\frac{3}{20}$

Teacher notes

The calculation above can be shown on a number line marked in twentieths:

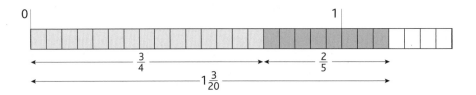

Diagrams such as this, on which you could mark decimals as well, help students to see fractions as numbers rather than just as symbols to be manipulated. This is a calculator unit and your main concern will be to help the students to become competent with their calculators at doing a range of fraction calculations. However, it will help develop understanding if you also encourage the students to look at fractions in different ways and to consider other methods of calculating with fractions too.

Students may have found the standard non-calculator methods difficult in the past, but, with the support of a calculator, they will be able to make sense of the methods.

They can also add and subtract fractions using decimals, changing both fractions to decimals and adding the two decimals.

So the calculation above becomes $\frac{3}{4} + \frac{2}{5} = 0.75 + 0.4$

$$= 1.15$$

Students should check that 1.15 is the same as $1\frac{3}{20}$

This example avoids the problem of fractions that convert to recurring decimals, but you may like to use the next example as a lead-in to Learn 1.3.

Example: Calculate $2\frac{2}{3} - 1\frac{4}{5}$

     a   using the fraction key

     b   by working in decimals.

     Compare the two answers and discuss the two methods.

Solution: **a**   The calculator sequence is $=$ 2 $a\frac{b}{c}$ 2 $a\frac{b}{c}$ 3 $-$ 1 $a\frac{b}{c}$ 4 $a\frac{b}{c}$ 5 $=$, giving an answer of $\frac{13}{15}$. Some 'textbook display' calculators will require a different sequence to enter mixed fractions.

     b   The calculator sequence is 2 $+$ 2 $\div$ 3 $-$ $($ 1 $+$ 4 $\div$ 5 $)$ $=$, giving an answer of 0.86666667.

     The two answers look different, but converting $\frac{13}{15}$ to a decimal shows that they are the same, but the first answer is exact.

Teacher notes

You could discuss different ways of doing this calculation as a reminder of the conventions for order of operations. If the second fraction were being added or if it were a simple fraction rather than a mixed number, no brackets would be needed; students should be able to understand why. It would be interesting to see what would have to be done differently on a simple non-scientific calculator that does not follow standard conventions for order of operations.

Students must be encouraged to keep numbers in their calculators, using the memory or $\boxed{\text{ANS}}$ key if necessary, rather than re-entering (less accurate) numbers from earlier parts of the calculation. It would not be efficient to convert both the fractions separately to decimals and then to add them up. Having said that, it is better for students to follow a longer route that they understand and can remember than to try to do something more efficient.

There is also the opportunity for students to gain some familiarity with recurring and terminating decimals and their fraction equivalents, but this is not covered formally in this unit.

Common errors

✗ Incorrect or inefficient use of calculator. For example, if students are doing a calculation such as $4 \div 2\frac{5}{8}$ by changing to decimals, they need to use brackets for $2\frac{5}{8}$

$4 \div (2 + 5 \div 8) =$

AQA Examiner's tip

Typically, examination questions on fractions, at both Foundation and Higher level, are poorly answered. In this calculator unit, make sure that your students know how to put mixed numbers into the calculator using the fraction button and how to convert between mixed numbers and top-heavy fractions. Many modern calculators give answers that are top heavy fractions. So if you type in 2.4 ▣, it would come up as $\frac{12}{5}$. Students have to be able to change this to a mixed number without a calculator as some will not do this for you.

 Learn... **1.3 Rounding**

You have already seen how to round numbers to decimal places. For example,

1.2832 correct to one decimal place is 1.3

1.2832 correct to two decimal places is 1.28

and to the three decimal places is 1.283

You also need to be able to round them to a certain number of **significant figures**.

12 832 has five significant figures.

Rounding it to three significant figures (s.f.) gives 12 800.

Rounding it to 2 s.f. gives 13 000 because 12 832 is closer to 13 000 than it is to 12 000.

(In each case the zeros are not significant figures because they only show the place values of the other digits.)

Note that zeros *can* sometimes be significant figures.

Rounding 1.2832 to 2 s.f. gives 1.3

Teacher notes

Students have to appreciate the two different roles that may be played by zeros in a number – as a digit like any other and as a placeholder to maintain the place value of the number. The following examples show zeros in both these roles. The zero in 6089.67 is a significant figure like any other digit in the number. When 6089.67 is rounded to the nearest 10 it is 6090. The second zero is not significant; it is used to distinguish between 6090 and 609. You could also discuss the zero in 510.49; when rounded to the nearest integer, the zero in 510 is significant, but when rounded to the nearest ten, the zero in 510 is not significant.

Rounding is a topic that all students should learn sufficiently well for it to become a routine part of their work, particularly when using calculators. In the exam, unless answers are exact or unless there is an instruction otherwise, students should round answers to three significant figures. Money should be rounded to the nearest penny.

Use of number lines such as those shown in the Student Book indicating the range of numbers that round to the same number will help students understand how and why numbers are rounded as they are.

It is also helpful to encourage them to focus on the 'decider digit' that determines whether the digit to its left is to remain the same or increase by one. When the number 356.84 is rounded to the nearest integer, 8 is the decider digit. When it is rounded to the nearest hundred, 5 is the decider digit.

Watch out for students who think that, if the decider digit is less than 5, the digit to its left should be reduced by 1 – such students need more number line work to see how the numbers relate to one another.

Example: Round the numbers **i** 510.49 **ii** 6089.67 **iii** 84.305 to:

    a the nearest integer

    b the nearest 10

    c the nearest 100.

Solution: **a**   **i**   510.49 is between the two integers 510 and 511. It is nearer to 510 because .49 is less than .5. So 510.49 to the nearest integer is 510.

       ii   6089.67 is between the two integers 6089 and 6090. It is nearer to 6090 because .67 is greater than .5

          So 6089.67 to the nearest integer is 6090.

       iii   84.305 is between the two integers 84 and 85. It is nearer to 84 because .305 is less than .5

           So 84.305 to the nearest integer is 84.

    Similarly for the remaining rounding; 513.49 is between 510 and 520 and so on.

    b   **i** 510   **ii** 6090   **iii** 80

    c   **i** 500   **ii** 6100   **iii** 100

Teacher notes

Rounding to decimal places is the same process as rounding to the nearest integer, ten or hundred, but some students find it more difficult if they are not confident in their use of decimals. Activities in which they arrange decimals in order, find numbers in between other numbers and work with number lines will help strengthen understanding. The following example encourages students to work creatively with numbers and realise that there is no limit to the number of numbers between any two.

Example: Write down four different numbers that to two decimal places give 3.52

    Look at the biggest number you have written.

    Find a bigger number that would still round to 3.52

    Find a bigger number that would still round to 3.52. How far can you go on?

Solution: The biggest number some students will suggest is 3.524. A bigger number that is still closer to 3.52 than 3.53 is 3.5241, or 3.5242 ... and then students can consider moving into the next decimal place and the next and so on and still be below 3.525, which would round up to 3.53. They should realise that the number of numbers between 3.524 and 3.525 is unlimited.

    Such a discussion makes a good lead-in to upper and lower bounds in Learn 1.4.

Example: From the following list, find a number that is the same:

    0.6594   6.594   65.94   659.4   6594

    a when rounded to one significant figure (s.f) as to one decimal place (d.p.)

    b when rounded to three s.f. as to one d.p.

    c when rounded to two s.f. as to the nearest whole number.

Solution: **a** 0.6594   **b** 65.94   **c** 65.94

Common errors

✗ Insecure knowledge of the place value and size of decimal numbers.

✗ Thinking that when rounding, for example, 78.3 to the nearest whole number, it will be 77 because you 'round down'.

✗ Confusion with zeros and whether they are significant or not.

✗ Difficulties when a nine is rounded up, such as when rounding 4.98 to one decimal place. The answer of 5.0 may need to be demonstrated on a number line to help students understand.

✗ Rounding up before the penultimate digit, for example, thinking 3.679 to 2 d.p. is 3.78

Bump up your grade

To get a Grade C, students need to know how to round to given numbers of significant figures.

 **1.4 Upper and lower bounds**

Continuous measurements can never be completely accurate and it is helpful to know how accurate they are.

Suppose that the weight of a person is measured as 62 kg to the nearest kilogram on bathroom scales.

This means that the weight is nearer to 62 kg than it is to either 61 kg or 63 kg. It can be half a kilogram either side of 62 kg.

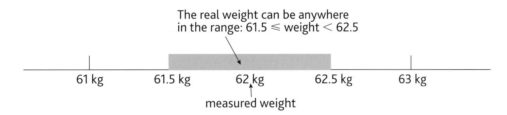

The real weight can be anywhere in the range: 61.5 ≤ weight < 62.5

61 kg   61.5 kg   62 kg   62.5 kg   63 kg

measured weight

If W kg is the weight, $61.5 \leq W < 62.5$

61.5 kg is the **lower bound** of the weight and 62.5 kg is the **upper bound**.

A weight less than 61.5 kg would be rounded to 61 kg.

A weight greater than 62.5 kg would be rounded to 63 kg.

Example: The weight of a man on the scales in a doctor's surgery is 84.6 kg, correct to the nearest hundred grams. What are the upper and lower bounds of his weight?

Solution: The weight is given to the nearest hundred grams so it must be nearer to 84.6 kg than to either 84.5 kg or 84.7 kg. It can therefore be as much as 50 g more or 50 g less than 84.6 kg.

So the upper bound is 84.65 kg and the lower bound is 84.55 kg.

If W kg is the man's weight, $84.55 \leq W < 84.65$. The weight cannot actually be 84.65 kg as this would round up to 84.7 kg. Hence the 'less than', rather than the 'less than or equal to' symbol.

Learn... 1.5 **Calculating with bounds**

It is important to consider possible inaccuracies in measurements when combining measurements. For example, a packet could contain 20 chocolate bars, each weighing 35 g to the nearest gram.

If all the bars weighed the least they possibly could, the lower bound of the total weight in the pack of 20 would be 20 × 34.5 g = 690 g.

If all the bars weighed the most they possibly could, the upper bound of the total weight in the pack of 20 would be 20 × 35.5 g = 710 g, which is quite a difference!

In calculating the maximum or minimum value of a quantity you have to think carefully about which bound to use: the upper bound or the lower bound.

If you need the **maximum** value:
maximum of $(a + b)$ = maximum of a + maximum of b
maximum of $(a - b)$ = maximum of a − minimum of b
maximum of $a \times b$ = maximum of a × maximum of b
maximum of $\dfrac{a}{b} = \dfrac{\text{maximum of } a}{\text{minimum of } b}$

If you need the **minimum** value:
minimum of $(a + b)$ = minimum of a + minimum of b
minimum of $(a - b)$ = minimum of a − maximum of b
minimum of $a \times b$ = minimum of a × minimum of b
minimum of $\dfrac{a}{b} = \dfrac{\text{minimum of } a}{\text{maximum of } b}$

Example: A room in the form of a cuboid has a height 3.9 m, a width 5.3 m and length 7.4 m, all measured to the nearest tenth of a metre. Work out the maximum and minimum possible values of the volume of the room.

Solution: The minimum measurements are height 3.85 m, width 5.25 m and length 7.35 m.

The maximum measurements are height 3.95 m, width 5.35 m, and length 7.45 m.

So, using a calculator for the multiplications,

the minimum volume is 3.85 m × 5.25 m × 7.35 m = 148.561875 m³

the maximum volume is 3.95 m × 5.35 m × 7.45 m = 157.437125 m³

Teacher notes

The result above is startling – over 8 cubic metres difference between the smallest and the largest possible volumes. Doing the calculation with the given measurements, 3.9 m, 5.3 m and 7.4 m gives 153.958 m³ so you would feel justified in giving the result as, say, 154 m³ but the calculations in the example show that this could be quite a way from the actual volume and we cannot even be sure of the result correct to one significant figure.

Students should be helped to realise the effect of accuracy and rounding on their work in the mathematics and science classroom and in manufacturing.

In this unit, students are required to deal with calculations involving addition, multiplication, subtraction and division of maximum and minimum measurements.

This is high-level work but students who are not always working at Grade A or A* level may find it easier to pick up marks on this topic.

 Common errors

✗ Thinking that if something is measured to the nearest 10 cm, it can be 10 cm either way.

AQA **Examiner's tip**

Always use the upper bound for maximum values. In the chocolate bars example this is 35.5 (not 35.4 or 35.49 or 35.499, and so on).

2 Indices and standard index form

Objectives

2.1 Rules of indices	Specification
C • use index notation and index laws for positive and negative powers including $10^3 \times 10^5$ and $\frac{10^3}{10^7}$	Interpret, order and calculate numbers written in standard index form. **N1.10h**

2.2 Standard index form	Specification
B • convert between ordinary and standard index form numbers • use standard index form for calculations	Interpret, order and calculate numbers written in standard index form. **N1.10h**

kerboodle! resources

k!   **Interactive activity: The laws of indices**

k!   **Learn: Significant figures**

k!   **MathsQuest: Identifying standard index form**

k!   **10 quick questions: Standard index form and indices**

k!   **Worksheet: Indices and standard index form 1**

k!   **Worksheet: Indices and standard index form 2**

k!   **Test yourself: Indices and standard index form**

k!   **On your marks…: Indices and standard index form**

Starter activities

Learn 2.1   **1**   Ask students to recall the square numbers up to 15×15 (and their associated square roots).

Learn 2.1   **2**   Ask students to recall the cube numbers of 2, 3, 4, 5 and 10 (and their associated cube roots).

Learn 2.1   **3**   Ask students to write their own definition of:
- a square number
- a cube number
- a square root
- a cube root.

Learn 2.1   **4**   Ask which is larger:
- 2^3 or 3^2?
- 3^4 or 4^3?
- 4^5 or 5^4?

Learn 2.1

5 Ask students to copy and complete the table:

	2^x	3^x	4^x	5^x
$x = 4$	$2^4 = 16$	$3^4 = 81$	$4^4 =$	$5^4 =$
$x = 3$	$2^3 = 8$	$3^3 = 27$	$4^3 =$	
$x = 2$	$2^2 = 4$	$3^2 = 9$	$4^2 =$	
$x = 1$	$2^1 = 2$	$3^1 = 3$	$4^1 =$	
$x = 0$	$2^0 = 1$	$3^0 = 1$	$4^0 =$	
$x = -1$	$2^{-1} = \frac{1}{2}$	$3^{-1} =$		
$x = -2$	$2^{-2} = \frac{1}{4}$	$3^{-2} =$		
$x = -3$	$2^{-3} = \frac{1}{8}$	$3^{-3} =$		
$x = -4$	$2^{-4} = \frac{1}{16}$	$3^{-4} =$		

Ask what they notice about the table.

Completed table is:

	2^x	3^x	4^x	5^x
$x = 4$	$2^4 = 16$	$3^4 = 81$	$4^4 = 256$	$5^4 = 625$
$x = 3$	$2^3 = 8$	$3^3 = 27$	$4^3 = 64$	$5^3 = 125$
$x = 2$	$2^2 = 4$	$3^2 = 9$	$4^2 = 16$	$5^2 = 25$
$x = 1$	$2^1 = 2$	$3^1 = 3$	$4^1 = 4$	$5^1 = 5$
$x = 0$	$2^0 = 1$	$3^0 = 1$	$4^0 = 1$	$5^0 = 1$
$x = -1$	$2^{-1} = \frac{1}{2}$	$3^{-1} = \frac{1}{3}$	$4^{-1} = \frac{1}{4}$	$5^{-1} = \frac{1}{5}$
$x = -2$	$2^{-2} = \frac{1}{4}$	$3^{-2} = \frac{1}{9}$	$4^{-2} = \frac{1}{16}$	$5^{-2} = \frac{1}{25}$
$x = -3$	$2^{-3} = \frac{1}{8}$	$3^{-3} = \frac{1}{27}$	$4^{-3} = \frac{1}{64}$	$5^{-3} = \frac{1}{125}$
$x = -4$	$2^{-4} = \frac{1}{16}$	$3^{-4} = \frac{1}{81}$	$4^{-4} = \frac{1}{256}$	$5^{-4} = \frac{1}{625}$

There are lots of patterns to be seen in the table and relationships between positive and negative indices. The table can also be used to demonstrate that $a^0 = 1$

Learn 2.2

6 Ask students to write down the number one million, one trillion, one octillion …
You can use the table below to help.

Name	US and modern British value	Traditional British value		Name	US and modern British value	Traditional British value
million	10^6	10^6		octillion	10^{27}	10^{48}
billion	10^9	10^{12}		novillion	10^{30}	10^{54}
trillion	10^{12}	10^{18}		decillion	10^{33}	10^{60}
quadrillion	10^{15}	10^{24}		undecillion	10^{36}	10^{66}
quintillion	10^{18}	10^{30}		googol	10^{100}	10^{100}
sextillion	10^{21}	10^{36}		centillion	10^{303}	10^{600}
septillion	10^{24}	10^{42}		googolplex	10^{googol}	10^{googol}

Plenary activities

Learn 2.1 **1** Ask students to recall the square numbers up to 15×15 (and their associated square roots).

Learn 2.1 **2** Ask students to recall the cube numbers of 2, 3, 4, 5 and 10 (and their associated cube roots).

Learn 2.1 **3** Ask students to write their own definition of:
- square number
- cube number
- square root
- cube root
- index number
- standard index form.

Learn 2.1 **4** Ask students to write down the rules of indices:

$a^m \times a^n = a^{m+n}$

$a^m \div a^n = a^{m-n}$

$(a^m)^n = a^{m \times n}$

$a^{-m} = \frac{1}{a^m}$

$a^0 = 1$

$a^{\frac{1}{n}} = \sqrt[n]{a}$

Alternatively, ask students to provide an example to illustrate each of the above.

Learn 2.2 **5** The table shows the distance of the planets from the Sun (in km). The information is given in standard index form.

Ask the class to place the planets in order of distance from the Sun, starting with the shortest distance first.

Planet	Distance (km)
Earth	1.5×10^8
Mars	2.3×10^8
Mercury	5.8×10^7

Learn 2.2 **6** Challenge students to write each of these populations in standard index form.

Rank	Country	Population
1	China	1 299 000 000
2	India	1 065 000 000
3	United States	293 000 000
4	Indonesia	238 000 000
5	Brazil	184 000 000

Learn... 2.1 Rules of indices

10^3 — Index (or power)

In words say '10 to the power 3'

Base

The **index** (or **power** or **exponent**) tells you how many times the base number is to be multiplied by itself.

This means that 10^3 tells you that 10 (the base number) is to be multiplied by itself 3 times (3 here is the index or power).

So $10^3 = 10 \times 10 \times 10 = 1000$

You can use the button on your calculator.

 125

Rules of indices

In general:

$$10^m \times 10^n = 10^{m+n}$$

$$10^m \div 10^n = 10^{m-n}$$

$$(10^m)^n = 10^{mn}$$

$$10^{-m} = \frac{1}{10^m}$$

$$10^0 = 1$$

Examples:

		Number	Algebra	Higher algebra
a		$8^2 \times 8^5$	$a^2 \times a^5$	$5a^2 \times 4a^5$
		$= 8^{(2+5)}$	$= a^{(2+5)}$	$= 5 \times a^2 \times 4 \times a^5$
		$= 8^7$	$= a^7$	$= (5 \times 4) \times (a^2 \times a^5)$
				$= 20 \times a^{(2+5)}$
b		$\dfrac{3^7}{3^2}$	$\dfrac{a^7}{a^2}$	$\dfrac{20a^7}{4a^2}$
		$= 3^7 \div 3^2$	$= a^7 \div a^2$	$= (20 \div 4) \times (a^7 \div a^2)$
		$= 3^{(7-2)}$	$= a^{(7-2)}$	$= 5 \times a^{(7-2)}$
		$= 3^5$	$= a^5$	$= 5a^5$
c		$(5^3)^4$	$(a^3)^4$	$(3a^3)^4$
		$= 5^{3 \times 4}$	$= a^{3 \times 4}$	$= (3)^4 \times (a^3)^4$
		$= 5^{12}$	$= a^{12}$	$= 81 \times a^{3 \times 4}$
				$= 81 \times a^{12}$
				$= 81a^{12}$

Teacher notes

Introduce students to the vocabulary of indices – single index but plural indices. Also make use of the words 'power' and 'exponent' when undertaking this work.

$$a^m \times a^n = a^{m+n}$$

This can be shown through a series of examples such as:

Example: $2^4 \times 2^3$ $\quad = (2 \times 2 \times 2 \times 2) \times (2 \times 2 \times 2)$

$\qquad\qquad\qquad = 2 \times 2 \times 2 \times 2 \times 2 \times 2 \times 2$

$\qquad\qquad\qquad = 2^7$

You can see that in the case of multiplication, it is quicker to add the indices.

$$\text{So } 2^4 \times 2^3 = 2^{4+3} = 2^7$$

$$a^m \div a^n = a^{m-n}$$

Again, this can be shown through a series of examples such as:

Example: $4^3 \div 4^2$ $\quad = \dfrac{4^3}{4^2}$

$\qquad\qquad\qquad = \dfrac{\cancel{4}^1 \times \cancel{4}^1 \times 4}{\cancel{4}_1 \times \cancel{4}_1}$

$\qquad\qquad\quad = 4$

You can see that in this case of division, it is quicker to subtract the indices.

$$\text{So } 4^3 \div 4^2 = 4^{3-2} = 4^1 = 4$$

$$(a^m)^n = a^{m \times n}$$

Example: $(5^3)^4$ $= 5^3 \times 5^3 \times 5^3 \times 5^3$

$= 5^{3+3+3+3}$

$= 5^{12}$

You can see that in this case, it is quicker to multiply the indices.

So $(5^3)^4 = 5^{3 \times 4} = 5^{12}$

$a^{-m} = \dfrac{1}{a^m}$

Example: $4^2 \div 4^7$ $= \dfrac{4^2}{4^7}$

$= \dfrac{\cancel{4}^{\,1} \times \cancel{4}^{\,1}}{\cancel{4}_{\,1} \times \cancel{4}_{\,1} \times 4 \times 4 \times 4 \times 4 \times 4}$

$= \dfrac{1}{4 \times 4 \times 4 \times 4 \times 4}$

$= \dfrac{1}{4^5}$

You can see that $4^2 \div 4^7 = 4^{2-7} = 4^{-5}$ using the laws of indices from above

$= \dfrac{1}{4^5}$

So $4^{-5} = \dfrac{1}{4^5}$

$a^0 = 1$

Example: $5^3 \div 5^3 = \dfrac{5^3}{5^3}$

$= \dfrac{\cancel{5} \times \cancel{5} \times \cancel{5}}{\cancel{5} \times \cancel{5} \times \cancel{5}}$

$= \dfrac{1}{1}$

$= 1$

You can see that $5^3 \div 5^3 = 5^{3-3} = 5^0$ using the laws of indices from above

$= 1$

So $5^0 = 1$

$a^{\frac{1}{2}} = \sqrt{a}$ and $a^{\frac{1}{3}} = \sqrt[3]{a}$

Example: $9^{\frac{1}{2}} \times 9^{\frac{1}{2}} = 9^{\frac{1}{2} + \frac{1}{2}}$

$= 9^1$

$= 9$

so $9^{\frac{1}{2}} = \sqrt{9}$

Example: $8^{\frac{1}{3}} \times 8^{\frac{1}{3}} \times 8^{\frac{1}{3}} = 8^{\frac{1}{3} + \frac{1}{3} + \frac{1}{3}}$

$= 8^1$

$= 8$

so $8^{\frac{1}{3}} = \sqrt[3]{8}$

In general, $a^{\frac{1}{n}} = \sqrt[n]{a}$

In terms of powers, it might be useful to know the prefixes used for numbers in the decimal system as follows (though this will not be required for the exam):

Prefix	Power	Symbol
tera	10^{12}	T
giga	10^9	G
mega	10^6	M
kilo	10^3	K
deci	10^{-1}	d
centi	10^{-2}	c
milli	10^{-3}	M
micro	10^{-6}	µ
nano	10^{-9}	n
pico	10^{-12}	p

Common errors

✗ A frequent error arises from the use of $2^2 = 2 \times 2 = 4$, as this often leads to the misconception that $3^2 = 3 \times 2 = 6$. In general, it is a good idea to avoid any work that might possibly highlight this misconception.

✗ Students frequently forget that the square root of a number has two possible answers, including a negative answer.

✗ Students often incorrectly believe that the cube root of a number has two possible answers, or otherwise can't deal with questions such as $\sqrt[3]{-8}$ which does have a solution, unlike $\sqrt{-8}$

AQA Examiner's tip

The answers $2^0 = 2$ or $3^0 = 3$ are frequent errors on examination papers. Students should be reminded that $a^0 = 1$

Students frequently confuse the laws of indices or otherwise forget the laws, such as:

$a^{-m} = \dfrac{1}{a^m}$ and $a^{\frac{1}{n}} = \sqrt[n]{a}$ and $a^0 = 1$

Learn... 2.2 Standard index form

Standard index form is a shorthand way of writing very large and very small numbers.

Standard form numbers are always written as follows.

a number between 1 and 10 → $A \times 10^n$ ← a power of 10

Converting from standard index form

To convert from standard index form to ordinary form, use the following information.

$10^1 = 10$

$10^2 = 10 \times 10 = 100$

$10^3 = 10 \times 10 \times 10 = 1000$

$10^4 = 10 \times 10 \times 10 \times 10 = 10\,000$

$10^5 = 10 \times 10 \times 10 \times 10 \times 10 = 100\,000$

$10^6 = 10 \times 10 \times 10 \times 10 \times 10 \times 10 = 1\,000\,000$ (1 million)

$10^{-1} = \dfrac{1}{10^1} = \dfrac{1}{10} = 0.1$

$10^{-2} = \dfrac{1}{10^2} = \dfrac{1}{100} = 0.01$

$10^{-3} = \dfrac{1}{10^3} = \dfrac{1}{1000} = 0.001$

$10^{-4} = \dfrac{1}{10^4} = \dfrac{1}{10\,000} = 0.0001$

$10^{-5} = \dfrac{1}{10^5} = \dfrac{1}{100\,000} = 0.00001$

$10^{-6} = \dfrac{1}{10^6} = \dfrac{1}{1\,000\,000} = 0.000001$

Converting to standard index form

To convert to standard index form from ordinary form:

Write your number in the form $A \times 10^n$ where A is a number between 1 and 10.

AQA Examiner's tip

Remember that 10^{-1} is the same as dividing by 10, and 10^{-2} is the same as dividing by 10^2 and so on.

Example: Write 405 000 in standard index form.

Solution: In this example, $A = 4.05$

$$405\,000 = 4.05 \times 100\,000$$
$$= 4.05 \times 10^5$$

Example: Write 0.00000060301 in standard index form.

Solution: In this example, $A = 6.0301$

$$0.00000060301 = 6.0301 \times 0.0000001$$
$$= 6.0301 \times \frac{1}{10^7}$$
$$= 6.0301 \times 10^{-7}$$

Teacher notes

Introduce the idea of standard index form as a way of representing very large and very small numbers. The mass of Saturn is 569 000 000 000 000 000 000 000 000 kg, which can be written as 5.69×10^{26} kg in standard index form. The size of an atom is 0.0000000000001 km, which can be written as 1×10^{-13} km in standard index form.

An alternative (and quicker) way of converting to standard index form:

Write 40 500 in standard index form.

Write 40 500

Place the decimal point so that A is at least 1 but less than 10   4.0500

Find n – the displacement from the decimal point   4 0 5 0 0

So $n = $ 4

$$40\,500 = 4.05 \times 10^4$$

Write 0.00000060301 in standard index form.

Write 0.00000060301

Place the decimal point so that A is at least 1 but less than 10   0.00000060301

          00000006.0301

Find n – the displacement from the decimal point

So $n = $ −7

$$0.00000060301 = 6.0301 \times 10^{-7}$$

It is also helpful to be able to carry out simple calculations involving standard index form without a calculator:

Example: Find $6 \times 10^8 \times 8 \times 10^{-3}$

$6 \times 10^8 \times 8 \times 10^{-3} = 6 \times 10^8 \times 8 \times 10^{-3}$

$\qquad\qquad = 6 \times 8 \times 10^8 \times 10^{-3}$ rearranging the order and collecting

$\qquad\qquad = 48 \times 10^8 \times 10^{-3}$

$\qquad\qquad = 48 \times 10^{8-3}$ using the rules of indices for $10^8 \times 10^{-3}$

$\qquad\qquad = 48 \times 10^5$ however, this is not yet in standard index form as 48 is not a number between 1 and 10

$\qquad\qquad = 4.8 \times 10^1 \times 10^5$ writing 48 as 4.8×10^1

$\qquad\qquad = 4.8 \times 10^{1+5}$ using the rules of indices for $10^1 \times 10^5$

$\qquad\qquad = 4.8 \times 10^6$

Example: Find $\dfrac{6 \times 10^8}{8 \times 10^{-3}}$

$$\frac{6 \times 10^8}{8 \times 10^{-3}} = \frac{6 \times 10^8}{8 \times 10^{-3}}$$

$$= \frac{6}{8} \times \frac{10^8}{10^{-3}}$$

$$= 0.75 \times 10^{8 - -3} \qquad \text{using the rules of indices for } 10^8 \div 10^{-3}$$

$$= 0.75 \times 10^{11} \qquad \text{remembering that } 8 - -3 = 11$$

$$= 7.5 \times 10^{-1} \times 10^{11} \qquad \text{writing } 0.75 \text{ in standard index form as } 7.5 \times 10^{-1}$$

$$= 7.5 \times 10^{-1 + 11} \qquad \text{using the rules of indices for } 10^{-1} \times 10^{11} = 10^{10}$$

$$= 7.5 \times 10^{10}$$

Common errors

Students frequently confuse the use of positive and negative indices. Stress that n is positive for large numbers (e.g. $40\,500 = 4.05 \times 10^4$) and n is negative for small numbers (e.g. $0.000000478 = 4.78 \times 10^{-7}$).

Students use the EXP or EE button incorrectly on the calculator and should be encouraged to become familiar with their particular calculator's functions.

AQA Examiner's tip

Students should watch out for how standard index form is shown on a calculator:

Writing

Input the number 2.61×10^4 as

2.61 EXP 4 or 2.61 EE 4 or

2.61 ×10ˣ 4

Reading

On some calculators, the display

2.61⁰⁴ or 2.61 04

should be interpreted as 2.61×10^4

Students sometimes copy the calculator display and leave this as their final answer, for example, 5 03 or 5 ⁰³ instead of 5×10^3.

Collecting data

Objectives

3.1 Types of data	Specification	
D • understand and name different types of data	Types of data: qualitative, discrete, continuous.	S2.1
C • understand the data handling cycle • understand that increasing sample size generally leads to better estimates	The data handling cycle – understand and use the statistical problem-solving process which involves specifying the problem and planning, collecting data.	S1
	Understand that increasing sample size usually leads to better estimates of population characteristics.	S5.9

3.2 Data collection methods	Specification	
D • design and use data collection sheets, surveys and questionnaires • understand and name other types of data collection methods	Design an experiment or survey.	S2.3
	Design data collection sheets distinguishing between different types of data.	S2.4
	Includes observation, controlled experiments, data logging, questionnaires and surveys.	S2.4
C • identify possible sources of bias	Identify possible sources of bias.	S2.2

3.3 Organising data	Specification	
D • design and use two-way tables for discrete and grouped data	Design data collection sheets distinguishing between different types of data.	S2.4
	Design and use two-way tables for grouped and ungrouped data.	S3.1
	Extract data from printed tables and lists.	S2.5

3.4 Sampling methods	Specification	
C • understand that increasing sample size generally leads to better estimates	Understand that increasing sample size generally leads to better estimates of (probability) and population characteristics.	S5.9
A • select and justify a sampling scheme and a method to investigate a population • use sampling methods including random and stratified sampling	The data handling cycle – Note: Higher tier candidates will be expected to choose suitable sampling methods and discuss bias.	S1
	Extract data from printed tables and lists.	S2.5

kerboodle! resources

(k!) Learning activity: Understanding the vocabulary

(k!) Interactive activity: Sampling methods

(k!) PowerPoint: Sample survey methods

(k!) Worksheet: Collecting data 1

(k!) Worksheet: Collecting data 2

(k!) Test yourself: Collecting data

(k!) On your marks…: Collecting data

Starter activities

Learn 3.1

1 Discuss a familiar situation with students, such as buying a mobile phone.

Ask them to imagine they had to gather information about the best models of phone.

Consider how each stage of the cycle would relate to this problem.

Some ideas are listed below, linked to each stage of the data handling process.

Stage 1: The student may simply pose the question 'Which mobile is best for me?' A more focussed starting point could be to ask, 'Should I use a contract phone or pay-as-you-go?'

Stage 2: Data is collected about available models and packages, their costs and other features.

Stage 3: The minimum requirement is to tabulate and summarise the data collected from Stage 2. They could use averages to compare the expected annual cost of a contract compared to pay-as-you-go, or they could include diagrams to show the cost of different models of phone.

Stage 4: A conclusion is drawn, which may be the end of the problem or may allow the problem to be refined. For example, the initial investigation may have shown that a pay-as-you-go phone would be much better. They can then carry out research in more detail, focusing on a research question or hypothesis about pay-as-you-go phones. Data is collected and the cycle begins again.

Learn 3.1

2 Divide the students into groups and assign each group a different part of the day to work with: Before school/During school/After school.

Ask each group to consider what data could be collected relevant to each of these parts of the day. Discuss the best way of collecting these data.

Allow the groups to compare their answers and consider whether there are any common elements, for example, there might be a need to collect common data on distances and costs.

Learn 3.1

3 This section does contain quite a large list of vocabulary for types of data. Many of these words will be unfamiliar to students.

Put the list of key terms that are relevant to this section on the board.

Different students then pick one of the key terms and, at the end of the lesson, in the plenary, the student will explain to the class their understanding of the meaning of the term from information they have learned during the lesson.

The terms are all to do with types of data and data collection:

- raw data
- primary data
- secondary data
- qualitative data
- quantitative data
- discrete data
- continuous data
- population
- sample
- sample size.

Learn 3.2

4 Ask the class (individually or in pairs) to list all the ways they can think of to gather data for a particular situation.

If students need some prompts, you could ask them to think about some of the following situations and consider how they would obtain data to address them.

- What is the current Number 1 download?
- How many buses run to London from your nearest town?
- What is the favourite takeaway food of Year 10 students in your school?

The students' answers can be linked to the part of the lesson on data collection methods. It will reinforce the features of each method the students must learn.

Here are some further ideas. In each case, ask your students what data collection is necessary:

- Catching a bus – times buses run/journey lengths/costs of fares/number of people travelling/comparisons with other transport methods.
- Sending a text message – data about number of characters used/price plans of phone/credit left in phone/cost of handset or package/contract/checking bars of signal/knowing number of person you want to send to.
- Having your dinner – cost of items/cost of different options/assessing known data about healthiness/calories in meal.

Learn 3.2

5 The students' answers here can be linked to the part of the lesson on data collection methods. This will reinforce the features of each method the students must learn.

Ask them to consider how much, and what type, of household waste is recycled, and design a draft questionnaire that would be carried out:

a for a face-to-face interview

b for a telephone interview

c for a postal survey

d for a survey carried out by email.

In what ways are the questions the same and in what ways are they different?

Learn 3.3

6 Ask the students to imagine that they wanted to find out whether males prefer dogs to cats and females prefer cats to dogs.

They should consider what questions would need to be asked in order to gain the information from a person. They then design a two-way table to collect the required information.

Learn 3.4

7 Challenge students to generate random numbers. They may think they can choose digits from 0 to 9 at random better than a random number generator such as a calculator.

Each student should write down what they think are 50 random digits from 0 to 9. It should be pointed out to them that a calculator can bring up 'random' digits almost instantly so students should write as fast as they can without thinking so that this is a fair test.

Then enter all students' results into a frequency table to see whether there is a bias towards a particular digit or away from a particular digit.

Learn 3.4

8 Collect 100 small stones and pebbles from a beach including 4–8 stones somewhat larger than the rest. (If you do not have access to a beach, any stones can be used but pebbles are best.)

Number the stones using a felt-tipped pen from 1 to 100 (do not order the stones in any way).

Before the lesson (to save time) find the mean weight of the 100 stones and keep a record of this.

Tell students they are going to choose 10 stones and that these should be representative of the whole population of 100 stones in order to obtain an estimate of the mean mass of the population.

Then 10 random numbers from 1 to 100 (obtained through calculator or equivalent) will also be used.

Which estimate, the student one or the random one will be better each time?

Whatever happens, there are many teaching and learning points to be had from this exercise and it is always a memorable one that can be recalled to cement learning.

This is a longstanding experiment, which usually shows that a random choice is better. It does need some preparation for the first time it is done but is an excellent classroom activity that is always very popular with and informative for students. It will take longer than a normal 'starter' activity.

Plenary activities

Learn 3.1

1 A A bar chart is drawn showing the percentage of households in each county that actively engage in recycling.

B The question is raised 'Which county in England has the best record for recycling?'

C The county with the highest % of households actively engaged in recycling is identified as the conclusion to the problem.

D Data is obtained from the internet about the % of households in each county actively engaged in recycling.

E Data is obtained by survey asking people which type of materials they recycle.

F A new related problem is formed – what types of materials are being recycled the most?

G A conclusion is drawn that it is glass that people are recycling most.

H A pie chart is drawn showing the proportions of all recycling that different materials make up.

Ask the students to put the aspects of the data handling cycle in the correct order. They refer to a problem relating to recycling around the country.

Answer: B D A C F E H G

An easy version of this is to have statements A, B, C and D only. To make it more challenging (as this means two journeys around the handling data cycle), also include E, F, G and H.

Learn 3.1

2 Match the terms on the left to the definitions given on the right.

Discrete data	The number of people or items in the sample
Secondary data	Data that cannot take exact values
Sample size	The complete set of items or people under consideration
Raw data	Numerical data that can be measured
Qualitative data	Part of the population under consideration
Population	Data that takes exact values only
Primary data	Data before it has been sorted in any way
Quantitative data	Data that someone else has collected
Continuous data	Data that cannot be measured using numbers
Sample	Data you have collected yourself

Learn 3.2

3 Ask students to find as many faults as they can with this questionnaire about the lesson they have just had on data collection methods.

1 Do you agree that this lesson was the best you have ever had?

Answer _____

2 How long did the lesson last? Tick a box.
  ❐ 0–30 minutes
  ❐ 30–45 minutes
  ❐ 50–60 minutes
  ❐ Over an hour

3 What do you think were the fundamental philosophies inherent within the teaching today?

Answer _____

_____

_____

_____

_____

Answers:

1 This is a leading question giving the opinion of the person asking the question within the wording.

2 There are 30 minutes in both of first two options, there is a gap from 45 to 50, and a mix of units (60 minutes and 1 hour).

3 This is complicated wording that few can hope to understand!

Learn 3.3

4 The following gives some data and a frequency table.

Data (time to get to work for 30 teachers in minutes)

8	12	7	21	19	17	20	55	23	7
3	17	27	10	32	6	8	21	33	6
25	7	12	11	9	34	22	20	37	18

Time, t (minutes)	Tally	Frequency
$0 \leqslant t < 20$	ⵏⵏ ⵏⵏ ⵏⵏ I	15
$20 \leqslant t < 40$	ⵏⵏ ⵏⵏ II	12
$50 \leqslant t < 60$	I	1

Ask the students to:

a criticise the **choice** of class intervals for the frequency table

b explain why the frequency table must have errors in it (and find what they are)

c design and complete a suitable and accurate frequency table for the given data.

Answers:

a *There are too few groups, and also a gap from 40 to 50. (Even though there is no data there, the classes must always be continuous.)*

b *Tally of 16 should be a tally of 17 and has also been miscounted as a frequency of 15. You can immediately tell there are errors as 15 + 12 + 1 does not equal the 30 mentioned earlier.*

c *Class intervals of 10 would probably be best, for example, 0 ⩽ n < 10*

Learn 3.3

5 Students should now be aware of the wealth of information contained within a two-way table.

Present students (in pairs or individually) with the following two-way table and see who can write down nine accurate facts from this two-way table the quickest.

Students from Year 10	Male	Female
On mobile phone	37	46
Not on mobile phone	21	17

Answer:

37 males on mobile phone

21 males not on mobile phone

46 females on mobile phone

17 females not on mobile phone

83 students on mobile phone

38 students not on mobile phone

58 male students were asked from Year 10

63 female students were asked from Year 10

121 students were asked from Year 10

Learn 3.4

6 Students should understand the two sampling methods that could be specifically tested in this specification.

Examination questions may ask students to suggest suitable sampling methods in order to address the functional skills standards or the data handling cycle.

Starters 7 and 8 for Learn 3.4 tested out issues around judgement sampling. Remind students about the dangers of using this sampling method.

Other sampling methods could be briefly mentioned to give students more options to discuss in an exam question.

For example, there is systematic sampling whereby every nth item from a list is taken. This is a quick and efficient way of obtaining a sample as long as there are no regular patterns in the data. There is also quota sampling. whereby items (usually people) are chosen by judgement until enough of each 'type' (such as male or female) have been obtained.

Learn... 3.1 Types of data

The data handling cycle is the framework for work in statistics. It has four stages.

The data handling cycle

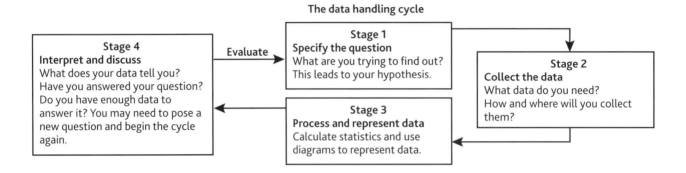

In any statistical project it is usual to go through the data handling cycle at least once.

The first stage is to decide on what you are trying to find out. This leads to the **hypothesis**, a statement that you want to investigate.

The second stage is to think about what data you need and how to collect them.

The third stage is to make calculations and summarise the collected data using tables and diagrams.

The fourth stage involves interpreting the diagrams and calculations you have produced.
This should lead to an indication of whether the hypothesis has been supported or not.

After completing the full cycle, it may be necessary to refine the original hypothesis and begin the cycle again.

The way you collect data, and how you represent them, may depend on the type of data you want.

When data are first collected they are called **raw data**. Raw data are data before they have been sorted.

Data can be **primary data** or **secondary data**.

Primary data are data that are collected to investigate the hypothesis.

Secondary data are data that have already been collected, usually for another purpose.

Data can be **qualitative** or **quantitative**.

Qualitative data are not numerical. These data measure a quality such as taste or colour.

Quantitative data involves numbers of some kind (a quantity).

Quantitative data can be **discrete** or **continuous**.

Discrete data means exact values such as the number of people in cars. They are numerical data that can only take certain values.

Continuous data are numerical data that can take any value.
They are always measurements, such as distance and time, which have to be rounded to be recorded.

Example: Ask students to copy the table and tick the correct boxes for these data.

Person	Qualitative	Quantitative	Discrete	Continuous	Primary	Secondary
Natalie						
Javed						
Petra						

1   Natalie collects data about the length of some famous cycle rides from the internet.

2   Javed asks each member of his class what their shoe size is.

3   Petra records hair colour of famous celebrities.

Solution:

Person	Qualitative	Quantitative	Discrete	Continuous	Primary	Secondary
Natalie		✓		✓		✓
Javed		✓	✓		✓	
Petra	✓		✓		✓	

Data are collected to answer questions.

For example, how many miles can a Formula 1 racing car run on one set of tyres?

You do not need to wait and see, others will have collected the data on this.

All the tyres of the same type should run for about the same number of miles.

The **population** of tyres is all the tyres that are the same type.

At some point a **sample** of the tyres will have been tested.

A sample is a small part of the population.

Information about the sample should be true for the population.

The **sample size** is important. This is the number of people or items in the sample.

It is important to think carefully about a sample size.

The bigger the sample then the more reliable the information.

So, the more tyres in the sample the more reliable the information.

However, it can be expensive or time consuming to collect data on a very large sample. You can't sell tyres you have used for testing!

Example: Bertie is investigating the question 'What is the average weight of a domestic cat?'

a What is the population for his question?

b Give an advantage of a large sample.

c Give a disadvantage of a large sample.

Solution: **a** All domestic cats (in the world).

b The larger the sample, the more reliable the results should be.

c It would be a time-consuming effort to weigh a lot of cats. It would be impossible to include all the domestic cats in the world.

Teacher notes

It is important for your students to be aware of the overall processes involved in the statistical analysis of a problem. That is, the bigger picture of the procedures for setting a problem, obtaining data, displaying and calculating with it and drawing conclusions from it.

Some of the questions in the examination could assess knowledge of the processes involved in the data handling cycle and there is much practice in the different parts of the cycle in the statistics chapters for Unit 1.

The beginning of this chapter focuses on the data handling cycle.

Use the first starter to familiarise students with the importance of knowing the data handling cycle as a basis for all work done in statistics. Some of the questions in the examination could assess knowledge of the processes involved in the data handling cycle and there is much practice in the different parts of the cycle through the statistics chapters for Unit 1.

The remaining focus of Learn 3.1 is then about types of data and a brief consideration of population and samples. Students at Higher tier will learn about specific sampling methods in Learn 3.4. Here, they should be learning about why samples are used and that on a basic level the larger a sample is, the more reliable it is.

However, students should also be made aware that a large sample is no guarantee of reliability. If the data collection method (Learn 3.2) is flawed, it does not matter how large the sample is, the data obtained will be worthless.

Common errors

✗ Not knowing the difference between the pairs of words that come together in this work, such as 'primary' and 'secondary' or 'discrete' and 'continuous'.

✗ Mixing up quantitative and qualitative. It may help to link the word 'quantity' with the former for numbers and 'quality' with the latter for features.

✗ Thinking that populations can only refer to people, and not appreciating that they can be objects or items.

✗ Thinking that a large sample is a guarantee of reliability.

AQA Examiner's tip

Students need to be familiar with the vocabulary of statistics. For example, the terms 'discrete' and 'continuous' are not well known among students.

Bump up your grade

Students who know their statistical vocabulary are more likely to get a Grade C.

 Learn... 3.2 Data collection methods

Writing a good questionnaire

One method of obtaining data is to ask people questions using a **questionnaire**.

Surveys often use questionnaires to find out information.

Questions can be **open** or **closed**.

  Open questions allow for any response to be made.

  Closed questions control the responses by using options.

It is important that questionnaires:

✓ are easy to understand

✓ are short and do not ask for irrelevant information

✓ give option boxes where possible

✓ do not have overlap or omissions in them where option boxes are used

✓ are not biased (such as 'Do you agree that …')

✓ avoid asking for personal information unless vital to the survey

✓ are tested before being used to show up errors or problems (this is called a **pilot survey**).

Example: A local councillor wants to know whether people will vote for him in an upcoming election.

He considers using one of these questions in a written questionnaire.

1 Will you vote for me?   Answer _____

or

2 Who will you vote for in the election next week?

❐ Labour   ❐ Liberal Democrat   ❐ Conservative

a What problems can you see with the two possibilities?

b Write a question that improves on both of the above.

Solution:

a As Question 1 is an open question, he could be given any response. People might just answer 'yes' or 'no' but they could say 'don't know', 'probably', 'might do', 'who are you'? Responses would be very difficult to categorise.

People are more likely to answer a closed question like Question 2. However, there are several issues with this question:

- There is no 'other' option for people who will vote for a different candidate – there are usually more than three candidates in an election.
- There is no box for people who will not vote at all – this could be quite useful to know.

b Who will you vote for in the election next week?

❏ Labour   ❏ Liberal Democrat   ❏ Conservative   ❏ Other   ❏ None

Teacher notes

There is quite a lot of learning to do here as there are so many different data collection methods.

See descriptions of these methods in the table provided in the Student Book on page 31.

You could split the class into small groups and give each group one of the methods from this table to focus on. Groups could read about the particular data collection method, perhaps doing some additional research if appropriate and if the internet is available during the lesson. Towards the end, students could report back to the rest of the class about what they have found.

Common errors

✗ Mixing up the different data collection methods.

✗ Not recognising that the wording of a question can have a dramatic effect on the responses obtained for that question.

✗ Not covering all options when designing questionnaire questions, for example, an option for 'other' or 'none' will nearly always be needed in a question.

AQA Examiner's tip

Students are better at recognising errors than writing questions themselves. They need plenty of practice at both skills.

Bump up your grade

Grade C students can write clear and unambiguous questions for questionnaires and surveys, and remember to include options for 'other' and 'none'.

 Learn... 3.3 Organising data

Sometimes when collecting data you need to design a **data collection sheet** or **observation sheet**.

These can be very simple. The key issue is that any possible item seen can be recorded.

Example: Niles is collecting data about the animals he sees in his garden.

He wants to see if there are differences between mornings and afternoons.

Design an observation sheet that Niles could use.

Solution: Here is one possible answer.

	Cat	Dog	Bird	Squirrel	Other
Morning					
Afternoon					

This table is an example of a **two-way table**.

Two-way tables are used to show more than one aspect of the data at the same time (time of day and animal). Two-way tables can show lots of information at once.

Example: Eggs are classed as small, medium or large and can be brown or white.

500 eggs are laid at a farm one day.

80% are white. Of the white ones 60% are large, the remainder are equally small or medium.

Of the brown eggs, half are medium and there are four times as many large brown eggs as small brown eggs.

Show all this information in a two-way table.

Solution: The table needs a row for each of small, medium and large, and a column for each of white and brown.

It may also be helpful to allow a row/column for the totals as this will help to fill the table in.

	White	Brown	Total
Small			
Medium			
Large			
Total			

Filling in the table can now be done systematically.

80% are white so $0.8 \times 500 = 400$ are white in total.

This means $500 - 400 = 100$ are brown.

60% of the white ones are large so $0.6 \times 400 = 240$ are large white.

The remaining white are equally small or medium which is $400 - 240 = 160$ then $\div 2 = 80$

Half the brown are medium = $100 \div 2 = 50$ are brown medium.

Of the remaining 50, four times as many are large as small. That is 40 large and 10 small.

	White	Brown	Total
Small	80	10	90
Medium	80	50	130
Large	240	40	280
Total	400	100	500

Teacher notes

This section focuses on the ability to convert raw data into tabulated data. The skills required range from simple tallying to the use and choice of suitable class intervals for a set of raw data. Students find it difficult to invent their own class intervals and should remember common ways of labelling class intervals as well as the rules regarding numbers of classes.

Common errors

✗ Failing to check that the total frequency in a frequency table matches the number of items of the original data.

✗ Going through the data counting all of one number instead of systematically going through the data one by one to ensure none are missed.

✗ Putting boundary values in the wrong section for grouped tally charts – look for which part of the double inequality has the extra line on indicating equality.

AQA Examiner's tip

Students must always remember to include a section for 'Other' in an observation sheet.

Bump up your grade

Grade C students check their two-way table values for errors by making sure that the sum of the row totals is the same as the sum of the column totals.

 **Learn... 3.4 Sampling methods**

Whatever method you use to collect data you need to consider sampling. Sampling is obtaining data from part of a population rather than all of it.

Collecting data from the whole population is called a **census**. This can be very expensive and time consuming.

There are a number of different ways to choose a sample.

Random sampling

For a random sample to be taken, every member of the population must have an equal chance of being in the sample.

The two most common ways of obtaining random samples are:

Use of random numbers

1 Number everyone in the population.

2 Obtain random numbers from a list or a calculator.

3 Match the people on the list with the numbers, ignoring repeats.

Use of a 'hat'

1 Write the name of everyone in the population on a separate piece of paper.

2 Put them all in a 'hat'.

3 Draw the required number out without replacing them.

Example: One student from the 29 in class 10A is to be chosen at random to be on the school council.

Briefly explain **two** methods which could be used to achieve this.

Solution: **Method 1** All the names of class 10A could be written on individual pieces of paper.

The pieces of paper could be put in a container.

One piece of paper could be drawn out of the container.

The name of the student on this piece of paper will identify the student to be on the council.

Method 2 Number all the students from 00 to 28 (or 01 to 29)

Use a calculator or random number table to obtain a two-digit random number. (If any number generated is larger than 28, obtain a further number until you get one in the desired range.)

The student matching the number obtained will identify the student to be on the council.

Stratified random sampling

Most data have some natural groups or strata within them.

For example, people are either men or women.

To get the best possible sample it is often useful to reflect any strata within the population.

So if a college has 70% male students, a sample should be 70% male to be as representative as possible.

For a **stratified random sample**:

- each group is represented by the same proportion as in the population. This allows you to calculate the *number* of items or people
- each item or person should be chosen at random from the group.

Example: One day 942 people use a sports club.

Of these 545 are members, 362 are guests and the rest are staff from the club.

A sample of 63 users from that day stratified by type of user is to be asked about facilities.

How many members, guests and staff should be in the sample?

Solution: **Step 1**   You are already given the total of 942.

Step 2   Fractions are $\frac{545}{942}$ for members, $\frac{362}{945}$ for guests and $\frac{35}{945}$ for staff.

Step 3   Multiplying each fraction by 63 gives a sample size for each group of

36.44 for members, 24.13 for guests and 2.33 for staff.

Step 4   Rounding these values gives 36 members, 24 guests and 2 staff.

Notice that 36 + 24 + 2 = 62 which is one short of the required total.

One of the values from Step 3 will need to be rounded up not down.

The value closest to being rounded up is the 36.44 for members so this should be rounded up to 37.

The final numbers for the sample are: members 37, guests 24, and staff 2.

Teacher notes

The sampling methods that students should be familiar with are random sampling and stratified (random) sampling. The term stratified sampling has long been used in examination questions though strictly speaking stratification is merely the way that the correct number of items or people in each group is determined. How these items or people are then actually chosen will still require a named sampling method – in the case of this specification that will be random sampling. Hence the correct name for stratified sampling is stratified random sampling. Students will not need to be able to demonstrate this level of understanding, however able students will benefit from a discussion about this issue.

Plenary number 6 briefly considers other methods of sampling which will enhance overall understanding of the topic. Students often feel that they could choose things 'at random' and if you have time to prepare and carry out the pebbles experiment, these ideas should be challenged (or they may not be as random is random!).

The second example uses stratified random sampling where the sample values come out as decimals and rounding is necessary. This is a popular question in examinations. The student book also shows a quick, efficient method to find the sample for each stratum when the numbers are friendly. Remember that sampling is Stage 2 of the data handling cycle, and exam questions may test what part efficient sampling takes in this cycle.

 Common errors

✗ Not rounding sample values in stratified random sampling (remind students to round to the nearest whole number).

✗ Believing random items can be chosen rather than using correct random sampling methods.

AQA Examiner's tip

Students need to practise obtaining the size of the sample for each group in stratified random sampling.

 Percentages

Objectives

4.1 Percentages, fractions and decimals

D
- compare harder percentages, fractions and decimals
- work out more difficult percentages of given quantities

Specification

Understand that 'percentage' means 'number of parts per 100' and use this to compare proportions.	N2.5
Interpret fractions, decimals, percentages as operators. Candidates should be able to interpret percentage problems using a multiplier.	N2.6
Calculate with fractions, decimals and percentages.	N2.7

4.2 Increasing or decreasing by a percentage

D
- increase or decrease by a given percentage

Specification

Interpret fractions, decimals, percentages as operators. Candidates should be able to interpret percentage problems using a multiplier.	N2.6
Calculate with fractions, decimals and percentages.	N2.7

4.3 Successive percentages

B
- understand how to use successive percentages

Specification

Interpret fractions, decimals, percentages as operators. Candidates should be able to interpret percentage problems using a multiplier.	N2.6
Calculate with fractions, decimals and percentages.	N2.7

4.4 Compound interest

B
- work out compound interest
- use a multiplier raised to a power to solve problems involving repeated percentage changes

Specification

Interpret fractions, decimals, percentages as operators. Candidates should be able to interpret percentage problems using a multiplier.	N2.6
Repeated proportional change. Including compound interest at Higher tier.	N3.3h
Calculate with fractions, decimals and percentages.	N2.7

4.5 Writing one quantity as a percentage of another

D
- express one quantity as a percentage of another

Specification

Understand that 'percentage' means 'number of parts per 100' and use this to compare proportions.	N2.5
Calculate with fractions, decimals and percentages.	N2.7

4.6 Finding a percentage increase or decrease

C
- work out a percentage increase or decrease

Specification

Understand that 'percentage' means 'number of parts per 100' and use this to compare proportions.	N2.5
Calculate with fractions, decimals and percentages.	N2.7

4.7 Reverse percentages

B
- work out reverse percentage problems

Specification

Interpret fractions, decimals, percentages as operators. Candidates should be able to interpret percentage problems using a multiplier.	N2.6
Calculate with fractions, decimals and percentages.	N2.7
Including reverse percentage calculations.	N2.7h

kerboodle! resources

- *k!* MathsQuest: Fractions and percentages
- *k!* Learn: Using percentage multipliers
- *k!* Matching pairs: Percentage increase and decrease using decimals
- *k!* Essential skills: Repeated percentage change
- *k!* Interactive activity: Percentages

- *k!* Watch out! Solving a reverse percentage problem
- *k!* Worksheet: Percentages 1
- *k!* Worksheet: Percentages 2
- *k!* Test yourself: Percentages
- *k!* On your marks…: Percentages

Starter activities

Learn 4.1

1 Use this to check whether students can find percentages of quantities. Display the spider shown (on the board or provided on paper). Write a figure in the body. Ask students to find the given percentages of it (this could be timed). For this unit, allow the use of calculators and include more difficult percentages if you wish. If you decide not to allow calculators, the exercise can be made quicker or slower by careful selection of the number you insert.

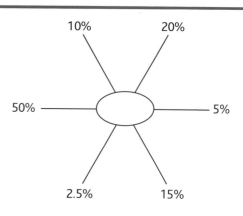

Learn 4.2

2 Set a problem that can be solved by a variety of calculator and non-calculator methods.

For example: A budget airline charges £68 for a journey mid-week, but 75% more on Mondays and Fridays. What is the airfare on Mondays and Fridays?

Students may find the 75% increase by:

- dividing £68 by 100, then multiplying by 75
- using the fact that 75% is equivalent to $\frac{3}{4}$ (dividing by 4 then multiplying by 3 or adding $\frac{1}{2}$ of £68 and $\frac{1}{4}$ of £68)
- using the multiplier 0.75

The result is £51 and adding this increase to £68 gives the increased value, £119.

(If your students are likely to work this out the same way, you could invent some 'pretend' students who work out the answer on the board using other possible methods.) After class discussion about these methods and any others that students suggest, introduce the most efficient calculator method, that is, including the original amount in the multiplier. In this example, the new amount is 175% (100% + 75%) of the original amount. So the multiplier is 1.75 and the new amount is $68 \times 1.75 = £119$.

Alternatively, use the similar example at the start of Learn 4.2 in the Student Book.

Learn 4.3

3 A common misconception is that you can simply add or subtract percentages in successive percentage changes. You could use Practise 4.2 Questions 9 and 10 as discussion examples to show that this is not the case. An alternative discussion problem is given below:
Jane invests £100 in a savings account that has a fixed rate of interest of 8%.

a How much does she have in the account at the end of the year?

She leaves the money in the account for another year. Again it increases by 8%.

b How much does Jane have in the account at the end of the second year? (£116.64)
Discuss the results: Where did that extra 64p come from?
Explain $100 \times 1.08 \times 1.08 = 116.64$

Learn 4.4

4 Check whether students can use the power key on their calculators by asking them to work out values such as:

1.2^4 (*Answer: 2.0736*)
1.03^6 (*Answer: 1.194…*)
0.7^3 (*Answer: 0.343*)
0.95^5 (*Answer: 0.773…*)

This could include rounding the answer (revision of work covered in Chapter 1) if you wish.

Points for discussion:

- Which numbers become larger when raised to a power and which become smaller? Why do numbers less than 1 become smaller?
- Multiplying by a number greater than 1 increases size (link to multipliers for percentage increases, e.g. mark-ups, VAT, interest)
- Multiplying by a number less than 1 decreases size (link to multipliers for percentage decreases, e.g. discount, depreciation)

- Why you can use $\boxed{x^{\blacksquare}}$ on the calculator twice for 1.2^4 but it is not correct to use it three times for 1.03^6?

Possible extension

Students use the inverse power functions to answer questions such as 'Can you find a number that multiplied by itself two times gives 10? 'Can you find a number that multiplied by itself three times gives 10?'

Learn 4.5

5 Give students some information to write as fractions (in their simplest form). This revises earlier work while also giving practice in the first part of the method for writing information as a percentage. A few possible examples are given below. To stretch higher-attaining students, include some with different units or ask them to make comparisons.

- I got 48 out of 80 questions correct. What fraction is this?
- 297 students out of 360 passed the test. What fraction failed?
- There are 12 boys and 16 girls in a class. What fraction of the class are girls?
- Each week Kate gets £6.50 pocket money. This week she spent £3.75. What fraction did she save?

These could be done with or without a calculator.

Answers: $\frac{3}{5}$, $\frac{7}{40}$, $\frac{4}{7}$, $\frac{11}{26}$

Learn 4.6

6 The table gives the average prices of some foods in 1991 and 2007.

Ask students (perhaps in pairs) to complete the table.

Food	Average price		Change in price	Change as % of the 1991 price
	1991	2007		
Large eggs (per dozen)	118	214		
250 g cheddar cheese	86	145		
1 pint milk	32	37		
New potatoes per kg	34	83		
Bananas per kg	119	87		

(From *Social Trends 39*, Table 6.19)

Answers: Eggs 96p increase, 81.4% rise, Cheese 59p increase, 68.6% rise

Milk 5p increase, 15.6% rise, Potatoes 49p increase, 144.1% rise

Bananas 32p decrease, 26.9% fall

Discuss the results, especially the increase of over 100% in the price of new potatoes and the percentage reduction in the price of bananas. Discuss possible reasons for the wide variation or perhaps pose the question: 'It is possible for prices to rise by more than 100%, but can they fall by more than 100%?'

Learn 4.7

7 Use an introductory problem to confront the most common misconception involving reverse percentages. For example:

Amy and Kate go shopping in a shop that is selling designer handbags at 20% off.

They look at a handbag that has a sales price tag saying £80.

Amy says 20% of £80 is £16, so the original price must have been £96.

The sales assistant says she is wrong. The handbag used to be £100.

Who is correct?

Discuss what causes the problem here. The reduction is 20% of the original price, not 20% of the sale price. So Amy is wrong and the sales assistant is correct.

Any Learn

8 Ask students in pairs or small groups to give definitions of key terms (any that are relevant to the work to be done in the session) and list examples from real life.

Discuss and select the best.

Plenary activities

Learn 4.1

1 In pairs or small groups, students position decimals and/or fractions at the positions of the equivalent percentages on a percentage number line. Each pair/group will need a percentage line and a selection of the decimal and/or fraction cards like those shown below.

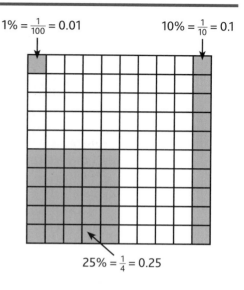

$1\% = \frac{1}{100} = 0.01$ $10\% = \frac{1}{10} = 0.1$

$25\% = \frac{1}{4} = 0.25$

Learn 4.2

2 Students do the following 'Which is larger? (or smaller if you prefer) questions. Allow them to use calculators.

  a 72 cm increased by 10%   or   70 cm increased by 12%
  b £140 increased by 30%   or   £150 increased by 20%
  c 54 kg reduced by 10%   or   56 kg reduced by 12%
  d £150 reduced by 50%   or   £125 reduced by 40%

Answers:
  a *72 cm increased by 10%*   **c** *56 kg reduced by 12%*
  b *£140 increased by 30%*   **d** *both the same*

Learn 4.3

3 A retailer's usual prices include a mark-up for profit. In a sale, it reduces its usual prices by a percentage that is 5% less than the mark-up. The manager thinks he should still make a profit.

Ask students to complete the table to see whether the manager is correct.
(If students find this difficult, suggest that they make up a cost price to help them.)

% mark-up on cost price	% reduction on usual price in sale	Overall % profit or loss
20%	15%	
25%	20%	
30%	25%	

How would you explain this to the manager?
Answers: 2% profit, break even, 2.5% loss

Possible extension

In the case of a 50% mark-up, can you find the percentage reduction that allows the shop to break even (sell goods for the cost price)?
Answer: $33\frac{1}{3}\%$

Learn 4.4

4 Mr McGregor says that the number of rabbits in his garden doubles every year.
Can students find how many times greater the population will be:

  a 5 years from now   **b** 10 years from now   **c** 20 years from now?

Answers:
  a *32 times bigger*   **b** *1024 times bigger*   **c** *1 048 576 times bigger*
Discuss how likely this is.

Learn 4.5

5   Students work out the answers to the questions and use them to fill in the percentage 'crossnumber'.

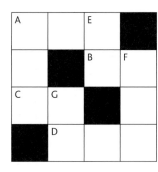

Across

A   Find 85% of 460
B   46% of the class passed the test. What percentage failed the test?
C   48 out of 75 people like porridge. What percentage is this?
D   115% of £540

Down

A   Work out 35% of £960
E $\frac{3}{20} = \dots\%$
F   210% of 210
G   391 out of 850 people travelled by bus. What percentage is this?

Answers: A *391,* B *54,* C *64,* D *621,* E *15,* F *441,* G *46*

Learn 4.6

6   Ask students to complete this table to show the percentage changes in the average price of phone calls over the period 2003 to 2008.

Phone	2003	2008	% change
Fixed	6.9p/min	7.4p/min	
Mobile: contract	12.7p/min	11.2p/min	
Mobile: pre-pay	15.9p/min	8.2p/min	

Answers: Fixed phone call prices increased by 7.2%

Mobile: contract phone call prices decreased by 11.8%

Mobile: pre-pay phone call prices decreased by 48.4%

Possible extension: use the answers to predict the prices in a later year (2013 is the easiest) and discuss how likely the predictions are.

Learn 4.7

7   Can students spot the reverse percentage problems in this mixture? You could ask students to list the questions that are reverse percentage problems in a plenary, then ask them to complete all the questions for homework.

a A t-shirt is reduced by 25% in a sale to £9. What was the price before the sale?
b There are 12 000 people at a football match. 28% are women. 15% are children.
How many men are there?
c A laptop is reduced from £495 by 20% in a sale. What is the sale price?
d A gas bill is £126.42 including 5% VAT. What is the cost without VAT?
e Akshata got 45 out of 60 in a maths test. What percentage did she get?
f In a school, 64% of the students are blonde. Of these students, 65% have dyed their hair. What percentage of students in the school have dyed their hair blonde?
g The number of fish in a lake is decreasing by 7% each year.
After how many years will the number of fish have halved?
h Three years ago, Ross invested some money in an account that earns $7\frac{1}{2}\%$ interest per year. He now has £795.07 in the account. How much did Ross invest?

Answers:

a *£12*	**c** *£396*	**e** *75%*	**g** *10 years*
b *6840*	**d** *£120.40*	**f** *41.6%*	**h** *£640*

Teacher notes

Students are allowed to use calculators in the examination for this unit. For this reason, most of the work in this chapter is intended to be done using efficient methods on a calculator. Non-calculator methods will be covered in the percentages chapter in the book for Unit 2.

Learn... 4.1 Percentages, fractions and decimals

1% (1 per cent) means '1 part out of 100' or 'one hundredth'.
It is equivalent to the fraction $\frac{1}{100}$ and the decimal 0.01. In money it is equivalent to '1p in the £1'.
To write other **percentages** as fractions or decimals, divide by 100.

35 hundredths

For example: $35\% = \frac{35}{100} = \frac{7}{20}$ or $35\% = 35 \div 100 = 0.35$ ← The figures move 2 places to the right

Use the fraction key on your calculator to simplify fractions, or the equals key.

To write a decimal or fraction as a percentage, multiply by 100 (the inverse operation).

For example: $\frac{3}{5} = \frac{3}{5} \times 100\% = 60\%$ and $0.7 = 0.7 \times \%100 = 70\%$

The figures move 2 places to the left

On your calculator press [3] [÷] [5] [×] [1] [0] [0] [=]

or enter the fraction $\frac{3}{5}$ then press [×] [1] [0] [0] [=]

Teacher notes

Remind students how to use the fraction key on their calculators to simplify fractions.

Here it may be useful to discuss the effect of dividing by 100 – moving digits two places to the right.

Example: Which of these is nearest in size to 58%? $\frac{3}{5}$ $\frac{5}{8}$ $\frac{11}{20}$

Solution: Write each fraction as a percentage:

$\frac{3}{5} = 3 \div 5 \times 100\% = 60\%$ This is 2% more than 58%

$\frac{5}{8} = 5 \div 8 \times 100\% = 62.5\%$ This is 4.5% more than 58%

$\frac{11}{20} = 11 \div 20 \times 100\% = 55\%$ This is 3% less than 58%

So, $\frac{3}{5}$ is the nearest in size to 58%.

There are many ways to find the percentage of a quantity. Here are just a few of them.

28% of £5 $= \frac{28}{100} \times 5$ or £5 $\div 100 \times 28$ or £5 $\times 0.28$

28 hundreths of 5   to find 1%   using a decimal multiplier   Try these on your calculator. The answer is £1.40.

The most efficient way on a calculator is the decimal multiplier.

To find a percentage of a quantity: divide the percentage by 100 to find the decimal multiplier.

Then work out: decimal multiplier × quantity

Example: Find **a** 32% of £65   **b** $17\frac{1}{2}$% of £7.99

Solution: **a**   Decimal multiplier = 32 ÷ 100 = 0.32

              0.32 × £65 = £20.80

         b   Decimal multiplier = 17.5 ÷ 100 = 0.175

              0.175 × £7.99 = 1.39825 = £1.40 to nearest pence.

Teacher notes

This section includes converting between fractions, decimals and percentages and finding percentages of quantities. You may decide to omit some or all of it with higher-attaining students, but it is likely to be needed by students working at the Foundation/Higher boundary.

Ensure that students have plenty of practice in using multipliers before proceeding to Learn 4.2 and encourage higher-attaining students to work out the multipliers in their heads.

Carrying out a check should also be encouraged whenever possible. In general, methods of checking include using an alternative method, reversing the calculation or estimating the answer. In situations where this is difficult or too time-consuming, just ask them to check whether the answer looks reasonable.

Common errors

✗ Thinking that 2% = 0.2 rather than 0.02 when using the equivalent decimal or decimal multiplier.
You could allow lower-attaining students to write 20% as 0.20 and 2% as 0.02 as this may help reduce their confusion.

✗ When a calculator gives an answer of 20.8, writing this as £20.8 though hopefully not £20 8p, or £20.08 at this level.

✗ Not rounding amounts of money to the nearest penny.
For example, giving an answer of £25.437 rather than £25.44.

✗ Doing calculations incorrectly.
For example, for 32% of £65, working out 65 ÷ 32 × 100 (reversing the 32 and 100) or 32 ÷ 65 × 100 (confusing this method with writing 32 as a percentage of 65).
Explain the stages in the working, that is, divide £65 by 100 first to find 1%.

AQA Examiner's tip

Students must remember to add a zero to values such as £18.5 to give £18.50, that is, they must use two decimal places (not one decimal place) for amounts of money.

Answers should be in pounds **or** pence – they should not appear in an answer together.
For example, £3.65p would be incorrect.

Students should be advised that when they are asked to put values in order of size, they should always use the given values in their final answer (and not those they worked out).

Advise students to use multipliers when finding percentages of quantities as this is the most efficient method.

Bump up your grade

Students need to be able to solve functional and problem-solving questions, which may be graded at C because of their complexity or lack of familiarity even though the underlying mathematical methods are more usually graded at D or lower.

Learn... **4.2 Increasing or decreasing by a percentage**

There are different ways to increase or decrease an amount by a percentage.

For example, to increase £86 by 25% you could do any of the following:

- Find a quarter of £86, then add it on:
  $\frac{1}{2}$ of £86 = £43 so $\frac{1}{4}$ of £86 = £21.50
  and the increased amount is £86 + £21.50 = £107.50
- Divide £86 by 100, then multiply by 25 to find 25%, then add it on:
  25% of £86 = £86 ÷ 100 × 25 = £21.50
  so the increased amount is £21.50 + £86 = £107.50
- Use the multiplier 0.25 to find 25%, then add it on:
  25% of £86 = 0.25 × £86 = £21.50 then add £86 to give £107.50

The most efficient way on a calculator is to include the original amount in the multiplier.

In this example, the new amount is 125% (100% + 25%) of the original amount.

So the multiplier is 1.25 and the new amount is £86 × 1.25 = £107.50

This is very quick to do on a calculator. The method is summarised below:

To increase or decrease by a given percentage:
- work out the new quantity as a percentage of the original quantity
- divide this by 100 to find the multiplier
- multiply the original quantity by the multiplier.

Advise students to work out the multiplier in their heads if they can.

Example: To decrease 38 500 by 6.4%

Solution: New amount = 100 − 6.4 = 93.6%

Multiplier = 0.936

Reduced amount = 38 500 × 0.936
          = 36 036

Use a different method to check:

6.4% of 38 500 = 38 500 ÷ 100 × 6.4
        = 2464

Reduced amount = 38 500 − 2464 ◄——————— Advise students to use the [ANS] key here
        = 36 036

Teacher notes

You could start this Learn by asking students to suggest ways of increasing £68 by 75% and discussing the advantages and disadvantages of each method. Students need to know that the most efficient way on a calculator is to use a multiplier that includes the original amount. The multiplier method becomes increasingly important in later sections of this chapter so give students plenty of practice with it now. Include multipliers that occur frequently in real contexts. For example 1.05 to include VAT at 5%, 1.175 to include VAT at 17.5%, 0.8 for a reduction of 20% and 0.7 for a reduction of 30%.

Encourage students to use a second method as a check. When using the second method shown in the example above, students should carry on the calculation, using the Ans key or a memory where necessary, rather than starting a new calculation. This avoids them having to key in figures again and means that they will be able to carry out any calculation they do as accurately as possible (only rounding off the answer at the end when necessary).

Common errors

Some of the errors listed in Learn 4.1 also occur in this section.

Other errors may also arise:

✗ Just finding the increase or decrease and not completing the calculation to find the final amount. Advise students to read the question very carefully and think about whether the final answer is sensible.

✗ Adding instead of subtracting when asked to decrease the amount by a percentage (or vice versa). Again advise students to read questions very carefully and consider whether the answer looks reasonable.

✗ Using an incorrect multiplier, for example, using a multiplier of 1.5 for an increase of 5%
Explain the multipliers:

in a multiplier of 1.5, the 1 gives the original amount and the extra 0.5 (½) is equivalent to adding 50%

and

in a multiplier of 1.05, the extra 0.05 ($\frac{5}{100}$) is equivalent to adding 5%.

AQA Examiner's tip

Advise students to read questions very carefully to find out if it is the increase/decrease or final amount that is required.

Students must use two decimal places (not one decimal place) for amounts of money.

Encourage students always to check that their answer looks reasonable.

Bump up your grade

For Grade C, students must be able to carry out more than one percentage increase/decrease. For example, a percentage price mark-up followed by a percentage reduction in a sale, or calculate simple cases of compound interest.

For Grade C, they may also need to be able to explain a method or error in working done by someone else.

Give students plenty of practice in class.

Learn... 4.3 Successive percentages

Multipliers give a quick way to work out the effect of more than one percentage.

For example, suppose you know that 56% of the 1250 people at a festival are male.

The multiplier for 56% is 0.56, so the number of males at the festival = 1250 × 0.56 = 700

If you also know that 35% of these males are under 20 years old, — Multiplier for 35%

then the number of males under 20 years old at the festival = 700 × 0.35 = 245

You can do all of this in one calculation:
The number of males under 20 years old at the festival = 1250 × 0.56 × 0.35 = 245

If you just want to know what percentage of the festival-goers are males under 20 years old, you just need to multiply the multipliers:

0.56 × 0.35 = 0.196 so 19.6% of the festival-goers are males under 20.

You can combine percentage increases and decreases in the same way.

Example: A school spends £6400 on computers. The computers depreciate in value by 30% in the first year and 15% in the second year. How much are the computers worth after 2 years?

Solution: The original price is 100%. In the first year the computers depreciate by 30%. This means the computers' value goes down to 70% of the original value.

The multiplier is 0.70 or 0.7 (use the first of these with students working at the Foundation/Higher boundary).

At the end of the first year, the computers are worth £6400 × 0.7 = £4480.

At the start of the second year, the computers are worth £4480.

After the second year, they are worth (100 − 15)% = 85% of this. The multiplier is 0.85

Count this as 100% now.

After 2 years, the computers are worth £4480 × 0.85 = £3808.

This can be done on a calculator in a single calculation:
Value of computers after 2 years = £6400 × 0.70 × 0.85 = £3808.

Also explain: 0.7 × 0.85 = 0.595   Multiplier for the first year   Multiplier for the second year

So the computers are now worth 59.5% of their original value – they have lost 40.5%.

Teacher notes

The introductory festival example above involves finding a percentage of a percentage. Encourage students to use the most efficient way by working out 1250 × 0.56 × 0.35 in a single calculation, rather than using the step-by-step approach. Writing 1250 × 0.56 × 0.35 is sufficient to show the working and by calculating it in this way, they avoid errors in copying intermediate values.

Also show students how to combine percentages even when they don't know the quantities involved. Students may need some practice with this type of question, before you move on to the computer example, which uses multipliers to combine percentage changes. You could explain this as shown above, but as before, advise students to do everything in a single calculation (as in the final line). Only one method, using multipliers, is given in the solution above (and in the student book) because this is the most efficient way to solve such problems and other methods are much more time-consuming. As a check, advise students to consider whether the answers they get look reasonable.

Common errors

✗ Misreading part of the question and increasing instead of decreasing or vice versa.

✗ Not remembering to add or subtract the percentage change from 100% when finding the multiplier for a percentage increase or decrease, for example, multiplying by 0.8, rather than 1.8 to find the result of an 80% increase. Advise students to always consider whether their answers are sensible. (If they make this mistake, they will get an answer that is less than the original amount, which obviously cannot be true after a percentage increase.)

AQA Examiner's tip

Advise students to read questions very carefully to find out whether it is the overall percentage change or the final value that is required. In examinations, it may help to underline or highlight what is required in the question.

Using multipliers saves time and also avoids the errors made when students miscopy intermediate values. This method also avoids inaccuracies caused by rounding values before reaching the end of the calculation.

Answers should be in pounds **or** pence – these units should not appear in an answer together.
Students must also remember to add a zero to values such as £18.5

Learn... 4.4 Compound interest

When money is put into a savings account at a bank or building society, interest is paid each year.

Usually the interest is added on to the **amount** already in the account (this is called 'compounding' or paying **compound interest**). For the next year, the amount of money in the account is greater so more interest is paid. This is an example of **repeated proportional change**.

For example, suppose you invest £500 in an account at a fixed **rate** of interest of 4% per year.

At the end of the first year you will have £500 plus 4% of £500, which is 104% of £500.

The multiplier is 1.04

Repeated use of this multiplier gives the amount in the bank after 1 year, 2 years, 3 years and so on. Each calculation can be done in one step on your calculator.

After 1 year, the amount is £500 × 1.04

After 2 years, the amount is £500 × 1.04 × 1.04 = £500 × 1.04^2

After 3 years, the amount is £500 × 1.04 × 1.04 × 1.04 = £500 × 1.04^3

If left in the account for 10 years, the amount would grow to £500 × 1.04^{10}

You can work this out on your calculator one year at a time or all at once.

For one year at a time:

Press ⑤ ⓪ ⓪ ⚌ ✕ ① ． ⓪ ④ ⚌ then ⚌ ⚌ ⚌ …… (count to 10)   Using the power key is more efficient.

To do it all at once, work out 500 × 1.04^{10} using the power key.

The amount after 10 years is £740.12, so the interest earned is £740.00 – £500.00 = £240.12

You can write a formula for the amount in the account after t years.

After every year, the amount in the account is multiplied by 1.04
So after t years, the amount has been multiplied by 1.04^t

An increase of 4% a year for 10 years leads to an overall increase of about 48%

So the amount in the account after t years is £500.00 × 1.04^t

Example: There are 950 deer in a forest and it is thought that the population is decreasing by 8% each year. Assuming this is true:

   a   what will the population of deer be 5 years from now

   b   after how many years will the population fall below 500?

Solution: **a**   The multiplier is 0.92 (because the population is reduced by 8% to 92% after each year).

Population after 5 years = 950 × 0.92 × 0.92 × 0.92 × 0.92 × 0.92

$$= 950 × 0.92^5 = 626.12$$

$$= 626 \text{ (to the nearest whole number)}$$

Using the power key is the most efficient way to calculate the answer.

   b   To answer this question, continue from part **a** and repeatedly multiply by 0.92, counting the number of times needed to reach a value less than 500.

The populations are: 626   576   530   488
    (after year   5   6   7   8)

After 8 years the population falls to less than 500.

Advise students to count years carefully and to carry on the calculation, using all the figures (not these rounded versions).

Teacher notes

You could start this Learn by looking at leaflets from banks or building societies and checking how much students know about saving and whether they are familiar with the key words used.

The calculations are introduced by taking a year-by-year approach. Students need to know how to work out amounts one year at a time, but there are some calculators that do not repeat calculations as described above. If any of your students have such calculators, they may need to press × 1.05 = at each stage. If you want students to list intermediate values, advise them to write down values to the nearest penny, while still keeping all the figures in their calculators.

If only the final amount is required, it is much quicker to calculate 4200 × 1.05^{12} using the power key. Discuss with students the advantages and disadvantages of each method and the complications that occur in real life. At this point, students may tackle similar questions on compound interest.

Students also need to be able to tackle calculations in other situations where the same percentage change occurs more than once. In the example above, the amount decreases rather than increasing. Note that if this example had just asked students to show that it would take 8 years for the population count to fall below 500, they would not need to find all the intermediate values.

The quickest way would be to work out 950 × 0.92^7 = 529.9 … then 529.9 × 0.92 = 487.5 …

This shows that the population is still above 500 after 7 years, but below 500 after 8 years.

Common errors

✗ Using an incorrect multiplier, sometimes by forgetting to add or subtract the percentage change from 100%, for example, 0.35 rather than 0.65 for a 35% decrease.

✗ Making errors when copying a lot of figures from the calculator. Advise students to round sensibly if they want to write down intermediate values, but that it is important to keep all the figures in their calculators for use in the next stage. Candidates sometimes miscount the number of repeat calculations needed to reach a target value. This is another reason for using the power method wherever appropriate.

AQA Examiner's tip

Advise students to use the index form where appropriate – this saves time and avoids the errors made when copying amounts. Candidates often waste valuable time by writing down unnecessary figures from their calculators at each stage. They should make sure that their method is clear, but then work out the answer in one calculation where possible.

 Learn... **4.5** **Writing one quantity as a percentage of another**

To write one quantity as a percentage of another

- Make sure that they are in the same units.
- Divide the first quantity by the second. This gives you a decimal (or write the first quantity as a fraction of the second).
- Then multiply by 100. This changes the decimal or fraction to a percentage.

Teacher notes

You could start this Learn by reminding students about writing one quantity as a fraction of another. Emphasise how important it is to write both quantities in the same units. So, for example, to write 50p as a fraction of £6, change £6 to 600p and write $\frac{50}{600}$. This can then be simplified to $\frac{1}{12}$. To change this fraction to a percentage, multiply by 100. Discuss with students possible ways of doing this all at once. Compare using the fraction key to enter $\frac{50}{600} \times 100\%$ with pressing $50 \div 600 \times 100\% =$

You can also include working in £: $0.50 \div 6 \times 100\% = 8.3333\ldots$

Example: The table gives the ages of children at a summer camp.

a What percentage of the children are 5 years or younger?

b Children who are older than 10 are permitted to go swimming.

    i What percentage of the children are permitted to go swimming?

    ii What percentage of the children are not permitted to go swimming?

Age (years)	Frequency
1–5	3
6–10	28
11–15	44
Over 15	9

Solution: **a** The total number of children = 3 + 28 + 44 + 9 = 84
So 3 out of 84 children are 5 years or younger.

Percentage of students who are 5 or younger = 3 ÷ 84 × 100 = 3.57% (to 3 sf)
or $\frac{3}{84} \times 100 = 3\frac{4}{7}\%$

↑
Divide by the total

b The number of children who are permitted to go swimming = 44 + 9 = 53

    i Percentage of children who are permited to go swimming = 53 ÷ 84 × 100%
= 63.1% (to 3 s.f.)

    ii The number of students who cannot swim = 3 + 28 = 31. Percentage of students who are not permitted to go swimming = 31 ÷ 84 × 100% = 36.9%

    Then 36.9% + 63.1% = 100% can be used as a check.

Teacher notes

As well as discussing different methods for writing 50p as a percentage of £6, you could also discuss the advantages and disadvantages of different ways of writing the answer. $8\frac{1}{3}\%$ and $8.\dot{3}\%$ are more accurate than 8.3%, but sometimes the fraction or recurring decimal may be much more cumbersome than in this case. In real contexts, it is usually not necessary to give exact answers and three significant figures are generally sufficient.

✗ Common errors

✗ Dividing by the wrong quantity. For example, if told that five students are absent and 20 students are present, thinking that the % absence rate is $5 \div 20 \times 100\%$
Advise students to think of the information as '.. out of ...' (in this example '5 out of 25' students are absent).

✗ Using the wrong frequency from a frequency table, for example, misreading part **b** above and either using the frequency of 28 or including 28 with the others in part **i** as this is the group that includes 10. Advise students to make sure that they select the right information from a frequency table.

AQA Examiner's tip

Candidates often forget to use the same units, use the wrong values or divide quantities in the wrong order. Sometimes these problems can be avoided if students are encouraged to think of the information they use in the form '.. out of ...' with the two quantities in the same units before doing the calculation.

Bump up your grade

Students may have to select relevant values from tables to work out the percentage required.

They may also be asked to explain a method or error in someone else's working for Grade C.

Learn... 4.6 Finding a percentage increase or decrease

To write an increase or decrease as a percentage

- Subtract to find the increase or decrease.

- Divide the increase (or decrease) by the original amount or write the increase (or decrease) as a fraction of the **original** amount.

- Then multiply by 100% to change the decimal or fraction to a percentage.

$$\text{Percentage increase} = \frac{\text{increase}}{\text{original amount}} \times 100\%$$

$$\% \text{ increase} = \frac{\text{increase}}{\text{original amount}} \times 100\%$$

Example: A skirt is 1.2 m long before it is washed. The length shrinks to 95 cm in the wash. What is the percentage decrease in length?

You may need to revise metric units with students.

Solution: Before washing the length is $1.2 \times 100 = 120$ cm
Decrease in length $= 120 - 95 = 25$ cm

Percentage decrease $= 25 \div 120 \times 100\% = 20.8\%$ (to 1 d.p.)

or $\frac{25}{120} \times 100\% = 20\frac{5}{6}\%$

Teacher notes

This follows on from the Learn 4.5 with the extra initial step to find the increase (or decrease) in the amount. Emphasise use of the original quantity in the calculation – the most common error occurs when students use the final amount instead.

Take the example of a holiday that goes up in price from £349 to £425.

The increase in price is £425 – £349 = £76.

Using the method from Learn 4.6, the percentage increase = 76 ÷ 349 × 100 = 21.77 …

This means that the increase is 21.8% (to 3 s.f.) of the original price.

The equivalent in fractions is $\frac{76}{349} \times 100 = 21\frac{271}{349}\%$

Discuss which of the alternative answers is most sensible.

Both of the examples above provide an opportunity to discuss rounding and also the advantages and disadvantages of giving the answer in terms of fractions. Answers given as fractions are more accurate than rounded decimals, but are often much more cumbersome.

The first example includes the conversion of units from metres to centimetres. You could show that the method also works in metres, that is, 0.25 ÷ 1.2 × 100% = 20.8%. Emphasise that whichever units are chosen, they must be used throughout.

In the case of this example where there is a decrease, using the multiplier method is more difficult. Dividing the final amount by the original amount gives 95 ÷ 120 = 0.79166 … To find the decrease, this must be subtracted from 1 to give 0.20833 … and hence the decrease is 20.8% as before. This is an efficient method, but only the highest-attaining students are likely to be able to use it successfully.

Common errors

✗ Failing to use the same units. As in the previous section, demonstrate how the use of different units leads to obviously incorrect answers.

✗ Dividing by the new quantity, rather than the original quantity.

AQA Examiner's tip

Candidates sometimes divide the wrong quantities in questions that ask for percentage increases or decreases.

Bump up your grade

For Grade C, students must be able to write a change in value as a percentage increase or decrease.

Students must also be able to explain methods or errors in work done by someone else.

 Learn... 4.7 Reverse percentages k!

In a reverse percentage problem you start with the final amount and work back to the original amount.

One way of working this out is by using the **unitary** method. It is based on finding the amount or cost of **one** unit (hence the name 'unitary').

Here the problem is solved by finding **1%**.

For example, a digital camera is priced at £156.72 in a sale. It has been reduced by 20%. What was the original price and how much is saved?

£156.72 is 80% of the original price (as 100% – 20% = 80%).

So, 1% of the original price = £156.72 ÷ 80 = £1.959

and 100% of the original price = £1.959 × 100 = £195.90.

The original price was £195.90

The saving is £156.72 – £195.90 = £39.18   (or work out 20% of £195.90)

An alternative method is by using the decimal multiplier.

In Learn 4.2 you started with an original amount and found the final amount by multiplying by the multiplier. To reverse the process, you just need to **divide** by the multiplier.

In this case the sale price is 80% of the original price, so the multiplier is 0.80 or 0.8

sale price = 0.8 × original price so original price = sale price ÷ 0.8

$$= £156.72 ÷ 0.8 = £195.90 \text{ (as before)}$$

Both the unitary and multiplier methods also work when amounts have been increased.

Example: After a $2\frac{1}{2}$% pay rise, Gary earns £7.79 per hour.

What did he earn before the pay rise?

Solution: 102.5% of Gary's original rate of pay = £7.79

Unitary method
1% of the original rate of pay = £7.79 ÷ 102.5 = £0.076

100% of the original rate of pay = £0.076 × 100 = £7.60

Multiplier method

Multiplier = 1.025

£7.79 ÷ 1.025 = £7.60

Advise students to check that their answer is correct.

To do this, they should increase it by 2.5% to get back to £7.79

This example shows that the multiplier method is a more efficient and powerful method if students can use it successfully.

Teacher notes

Use a familiar situation such as buying trousers in a sale to explain the possible methods to students. The unitary and multiplier methods are summarised below.

Unitary method	**Multiplier method**
Work out the new percentage of the original price.	Divide by the multiplier.

Divide by this to find 1%

Multiply by 100 to find 100%

The multiplier is a powerful and efficient method, especially if students are able to work out the multiplier in their heads.

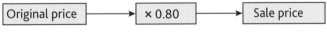

20% reduction, means sale price is 80%

Original price ⟶ × 0.80 ⟶ Sale price

To find the original price, reverse the process

Original price ⟵ ÷ 0.80 ⟵ Sale price

Original price = £156.72 ÷ 0.80 = £195.90

Whichever method is used, advise students to check that their answer is correct. In this example, reducing £195.90 by 20% takes you back to £156.72.

Common errors

✗ Not remembering that the given percentage is a percentage of the **original** amount.

✗ Trying to reverse a percentage decrease by adding the given percentage of the final amount.

AQA Examiner's tip

Many candidates fail to recognise reverse percentage problems. They often think that they can reverse a percentage increase by subtracting the given percentage of the final amount (or reverse a percentage decrease by adding the given percentage of the final amount).

Ratio and proportion

Objectives

5.1 Finding and simplifying ratios	Specification
D • use ratio notation, including reduction to its simplest form and its links to fraction notation	Use ratio notation, including reduction to its simplest form and its various links to fraction notation. **N3.1**

5.2 Using ratios to find quantities	Specification
D • divide a quantity in a given ratio • solve simple ratio and proportion problems, such as finding the ratio of teachers to students in a school	Solve problems involving ratio and proportion. **N3.3**
C • solve more complex ratio and proportion problems such as sharing money in the ratio of people's ages	

5.3 The unitary method	Specification
C • solve ratio and proportion problems using the unitary method	Solve problems involving ratio and proportion, including the unitary method of solution. **N3.3**

kerboodle! resources

k! Interactive activity: Ratios

k! Matching pairs: Using ratios to find quantities

k! PowerPoint: Solve problems involving proportion

k! Worksheet: Ratio and proportion 1

k! Worksheet: Ratio and proportion 2

k! Test yourself: Ratio

k! On your marks…: Ratio and proportion

Starter activities

Learn 5.1

1 Give students a fraction that can be simplified and ask them to give you its simplest form (on mini-whiteboards so that everyone participates and you can see all the answers) as quickly as they can. Check for students who are unable to start, those who are making errors, those who have not simplified fractions fully and so on, and sort out difficulties before moving on to the next fraction.

2 Show students a number such as one from the list below. Ask them to list all the factors of the number shown. Check for omissions, errors, incomplete answers and so on, and deal with difficulties before giving the next number. Choose the next number according to responses to the first. Discuss divisibility and ask: How can you tell when a number is divisible by 2, 10, 5, 3, …?

Examples of possible numbers to discuss: 36, 70, 80, 108, 144, 1000

Learn 5.2

3 Give each group of students a number of cubes or similar items and ask them to split these into two groups in a certain ratio – for example, 30 cubes to be split into two groups so that one has twice as many cubes as the other. Some students will be able to do this straight away; others may need to put two cubes in the first group and one in the second until all the cubes are allocated.

Vary the difficulty of the number of cubes and the ratios to suit the students and the progress they make. As the activity develops, encourage the use of ratio notation, and ask students to do the problems without using the cubes. Those who progress well can help others who need support and suggest further challenges.

Discuss methods and which numbers are easy to split into which ratios and so on, before going on to the more formal main part of the lesson and written questions.

Learn 5.3

4   In preparation for using the unitary method, ask questions such as:
- If three cups of coffee cost £4.50, what is the cost of one cup of coffee?
- If 20 litres of diesel cost £19.20, what does 1 litre cost?
- It costs £32.50 for five theatre tickets; how much is one ticket?
- If three people take a month to complete a contract, how long would one person take?
- Renting a holiday cottage for four people costs £250; how much does it cost for one person?

Students should recognise that the final example is very unlikely to be soluable by the unitary method!

Encourage a functional approach by discussing methods, use (or not) of calculator, when you have to multiply and when divide, when an answer cannot be found and so on. The students may be able to suggest other examples for discussion.

Plenary activities

Learn 5.1

1   You could do this as a demonstration or by students in pairs or small groups. Take two pieces of A4 paper (or a larger A size if available). Two different colours provide opportunities for an attractive display. Cut one piece in half parallel to the shorter sides and turn one of the halves round to show that its sides are in the same ratio as the original piece. Check by measurement also. Repeat the halving, showing that the ratio is always the same. Encourage students to discuss what they see, explain the relationships between the lengths and the areas of the different sizes and so on.

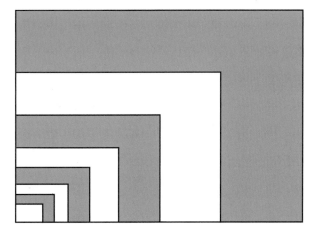

(There are possibilities for some more advanced work here – students can show algebraically that the ratio of the lengths of the sides of A sizes of paper is $1 : \sqrt{2}$. The additional information that A0 is 1 square metre enables the measurements of each size to be calculated.)

Learn 5.2

2   Ask students to spend a couple of minutes thinking of some difficult examples of splitting quantities according to a given ratio. Choose students to come out to work through their examples on the board and discuss the issues that arise. This would be appropriate in a lesson in which you had used Starter 4 at the beginning.

Learn 5.3

3   Get students to generate a combined 'mind map' of what they now know about ratio, following individual thought and pair discussion.

Learn... 5.1 Finding and simplifying ratios

Ratios are a good way of comparing quantities such as the number of teachers in a school and the number of students.

The colon symbol is used to express ratio.

In a school with 50 teachers and 800 students, the teacher : student ratio is 50 : 800

You read 50 : 800 as '50 to 800'.

Ratios can be simplified like fractions.

Each number has been divided by 10

Ratio = 50 : 800 = 5 : 80 = 1 : 16

Each number has been divided by 5

This is just like simplifying fractions $\dfrac{50}{800} = \dfrac{5}{80} = \dfrac{1}{16}$

$\div 10 \quad \div 5$

$\div 10 \quad \div 5$

Ratios with 1 on one side are called unitary ratios.

Remember that you can use your calculator to simplify fractions by pressing the $\boxed{=}$ button.

The simplest form of the ratio 50 : 800 is 1 : 16, just as the simplest fraction equivalent to $\dfrac{50}{800}$ is $\dfrac{1}{16}$

This means there is one teacher for every 16 students, and $\dfrac{1}{16}$ of a teacher for every student.

The proportion of teachers in the school is $\dfrac{1}{17}$ and the proportion of students is $\dfrac{16}{17}$

Example: In a survey, 2000 people said whether or not they thought the monarchy should be abolished.

Should the monarchy be abolished?	
Yes	No
1040	960

What is the ratio of yes votes : no votes in its simplest form?

Solution: The ratio is 1040 : 960, which simplifies to 13 : 12.

The ratio can be simplified by hand or on a calculator. Using the calculator fraction key is the sensible way for this unit.

The numbers have to be put into the calculator the 'wrong' way round in order to avoid getting a mixed number for the answer – this would be a useful discussion point.

Teacher notes

It is important that students understand ratio and how it is linked with fractions, decimals and percentages.

Develop confidence and understanding by using as many everyday examples as possible.

Examples such as how many miles per gallon a car can go show that in some circumstances it is quite correct for ratios to have units in; this point is worth exploring.

Most ratio questions can be solved in a number of ways; encourage students to explore different methods, explain them to others, and discuss their advantages and disadvantages.

Common errors

Errors that students make with fractions may also occur with ratios.

✗ Using adding and subtracting to simplify ratios instead of multiplying and dividing.

✗ Lack of familiarity with the fraction key ($a\frac{b}{c}$ or ▦) on calculator.

✗ Students may confuse the numbers in the ratio with the 'actual' numbers in the calculations, such as assuming that if the ratio of boys to girls is 12:13 there must be 12 boys and 13 girls.

AQA *Examiner's tip*

A common mistake is to write a ratio using different units. Encourage students to check that the units are the same.

Students may be asked to comment on the advantages and disadvantages of different methods in the examination.

 Learn... **5.2   Using ratios to find quantities**

You can use ratios to find numbers and quantities.

You can find:

■ the number of boys and the number of girls in a school

if you know

■ the ratio of boys to girls

and

■ the total number of students.

For example, in a school of 1000 students, the ratio of boys to girls is 9:11

This means that for every 9 boys there are 11 girls, whatever the size of the school.

9 + 11 = 20, so

9 out of every 20 students are boys so $\frac{9}{20}$ of the students are boys.

11 out of every 20 students are girls so $\frac{11}{20}$ of the students are girls.

The school has 1000 students, so to find the number of boys, work out $\frac{9}{20}$ of 1000.

To find the number of girls work out $\frac{11}{20}$ of 1000.

$\frac{1}{20}$ of 1000 = 1000 ÷ 20 = 50

Number of boys = 50 × 9 = 450

Number of girls = 50 × 11 = 550

Example: The three investors in a business put in money in the ratio 1:1:3. How much does each investor receive when the profits of £35 624 are shared in the ratio of investments?

Solution: The total number of shares is 1 + 1 + 3 = 5

So, the first two investors each receive $\frac{1}{5}$ of the profits and the third receives $\frac{3}{5}$

$\frac{1}{5}$ of 35 624 = 35 624 ÷ 5 = 7124.8

$\frac{3}{5}$ of 35 624 = 7124.8 × 3 = 21 374.4

So the investors receive £7124.80, £7124.80 and £21 374.40.

Teacher notes

The method above is a standard one and links well with the unitary method that follows.

You may also wish to discuss using fractions (finding the third investor's share by finding $\frac{3}{5}$ of £35 624) to remind students of fraction calculations. This can easily be done using the fraction key $a\frac{b}{c}$ or ▦ on the calculator; it is worthwhile allowing students to explore different ways of doing the calculation as some may think that you have to divide by $\frac{3}{5}$, or not realise that it does not matter in which order you divide by 5 and multiply by 3, provided that both division by 5 and multiplication by 3 take place.

Common errors

✗ Lack of understanding of and competence with the ideas of finding fractions of quantities.

✗ Thinking that you have to divide to find a fraction of something. For example, to find $\frac{1}{3}$ of 10, doing the calculation $10 \div \frac{1}{3}$ rather than $10 \times \frac{1}{3}$

AQA Examiner's tip

Students can eliminate some sources of error by checking that answers are sensible and consistent; in this section, they should check that the separate shares add up to the total amount being shared.

Bump up your grade

To get a Grade C, students have to be able to work with ratios in practical situations.

Learn... 5.3 The unitary method

You can use the **unitary method** to do all types of percentages as well as ratio and proportion. The method is based on finding the amount or cost of **one** unit (hence the name 'unitary').

So if you know how much 20 litres of petrol cost, you can find the cost of one litre and then the cost of any number of litres.

Example: Amy drives for 4 hours on the motorway and covers 180 miles. How far will she travel if she travels for 6 hours at the same average speed?

Solution: In 4 hours, Amy travels 180 miles.

In 1 hour, she travels $\frac{180}{4}$ miles.

In 6 hours, she will travel 6 miles $\times \frac{180}{4} = 270$ miles.

Teacher notes

This is a very important section; the unitary method is essential for mathematical functionality. Give students the opportunity to think of and work on simple examples such as finding the cost of five cups of coffee given the cost of three so that they can gain understanding of the process and practise it.

All distance/time questions at GCSE level such as the example above can be solved by using the unitary method. As this is a calculator unit, you could provide some realistic data to work with so that students can easily check that answers are sensible.

'Best buy' type questions can be worked out by the unitary method both ways round: how much does one unit of the product cost (the cost of 1 g, for example) or how much of it you can get for unit cost (what weight you can by for £1, for example). Both are equally valid and worthy of discussion.

Common errors

✗ Difficulties with working with fractions.

✗ Not applying common sense to working out the quantities; trying to use a 'rule' instead.

✗ Not knowing whether to expect an answer that is bigger or smaller than the original amount.

✗ Not realising that dividing a quantity by a number between 0 and 1 will produce a bigger answer.

AQA Examiner's tip

Encourage students to make sure that their answers make sense; 15 calculators should obviously cost more than six, and a simple estimation should help check that the answer is reasonable.

Bump up your grade

Students must be able to use the unitary method to be confident with Grade C questions.

 **Statistical measures**

Objectives

6.1 Frequency distributions	Specification	
D • calculate the mean for a frequency distribution	Calculate median, mean, range, mode and modal class.	**S3.3**
	Compare distributions and make inferences.	**S4.4**

6.2 Grouped frequency distributions	Specification	
D • find the modal class for grouped data	Calculate median, mean, range, mode and modal class.	**S3.3**
C • find the mean for grouped data	Calculate median, mean, range, mode and modal class	**S3.3**
• find the median class for grouped data	Compare distributions and make inferences.	**S4.4**
B • find the upper and lower quartiles and calculate the inter-quartile range for a frequency distribution	Quartiles and inter-quartile range.	**S3.3h**

kerboodle! resources

- (k!) Watch out!: Finding the mean
- (k!) PowerPoint: Frequency tables and the mean
- (k!) Matching pairs: Averages
- (k!) MathsQuest: Finding the median for a frequency table
- (k!) 10 quick questions: Statistical measures
- (k!) Interactive activity: Estimating the mean for a grouped frequency distribution

- (k!) Matching pairs: Midpoints
- (k!) Worksheet: Statistical measures 1
- (k!) Worksheet: Statistical measures 2
- (k!) Test yourself: Finding the mean for a frequency distribution
- (k!) On your marks...: Statistical measures

Starter activities

Learn 6.1

1 Discuss the strengths and weaknesses of each of the mean, median and mode.

Consolidation of why each measure is used, as well as how it is used, is important for understanding.

Learn 6.1

2 Students should be able to think about the circumstances in which using different types of average are the most beneficial. This will help them prepare for the chapter by recapping on the meaning of and strengths of the measures of average.

For this starter, give each student three cards, one with mean written on it, one with mode and one with median.

Alternatively, students could write on mini-whiteboards.

For each of the following situations, students should hold up the appropriate card for the measure of average they think is the most suitable for an 'average' in each of these contexts.

a finding the average pocket money for the class

b finding the average shoe size for people

c finding the average speed of cars on a motorway

d finding the average time it takes students to get to school

e finding the average price of a house in the UK

For some of the above, more than one measure may be appropriate.

Answers:

a *mean or median, if some high values occur*

b *mode, as the most common size would need to be produced in the largest quantity*

c *mean or median*

d *mean*

e *median, some very high values would possibly skew the mean*

This activity could be extended or perhaps made easier by introducing values.

For example, if the pocket money of 10 students was £5, £6, £8, £6, £7, £10, £5, £7, £8, £7, which measure of average might be best to use?

However, if the pocket money of 10 students was £5, £6, £8, £6, £7, £10, £5, £7, £8, £48, which measure would be best now?

| Learn 6.1 |

3 Ask the following questions:

The mean/median/mode of two numbers is 20. What could the numbers be?

The mean/median/mode of three numbers is 10. What could the three numbers be?

The mean/median/mode of four numbers is 50. What could the four numbers be?

How many possible answers do students think there are to each of these puzzles?

Students can make up some puzzles of their own similar to these.

| Learn 6.1 |

4 Students should pair up to roll two dice on 20 occasions. One student rolls the dice and the other records the total of the two dice when they are added together.

Firstly, find the measures of average for the raw data.

Then team up three pairs of students to combine their data into a frequency distribution. Once the frequency distribution is complete, students should find the measures of average for the combined distribution. Which of these measures is the same as the respective average of the individual measures for the three pairs of students?

This process could be repeated as a Plenary with the dice scores being multiplied instead of added.

| Learn 6.2 |

5 As a class, students should choose some of the following data to collect about themselves and their classmates:

Height*, Arm Span*, Foot length*, hair colour, eye colour, method of getting to school, time to get to school*.

Ensure that at least two of the starred topics are included to give students some further practice at grouping data themselves (revision of Chapter 3).

Which averages are suitable for these variables?

Ensure that students are aware that they will need to group the starred data (ask them why).

Calculate estimates for these averages or find the group in which they lie.

Plenary activities

Learn 6.1

1 In examinations, students often confuse the three measures of average.

Traditionally hints such as meDian = miDdle or mOde = mOst have been used in an attempt to remember the difference between each type of average.

Can students come up with some clever or memorable ways of helping some of their classmates to remember which average is which?

Learn 6.1

2 Ask: Can any of the measures of average have a value equal to the highest value of the data?

Answer: all three

Method: Write down a set of data where the mean is the same as the highest value.

Write down a set of data where the mode and median are the same as the highest value but the mean is less than the highest value.

Write down a set of data where the mode is also the highest value but the median and the mean are less than the highest value.

Students should try to write some of their answers in frequency distribution tables, such as the one in Plenary 3.

Value	Frequency
2	4
5	10
8	14
11	12

Learn 6.1

3 Ask students to find the mean of 2, 5, 8 and 11.

Now ask them to find the mean of this frequency distribution.

How did they know that the answer to the second question would be greater than the answer to the first question?

Learn 6.1

4 Students should pair up to roll two dice on 20 occasions. One student rolls the dice, and the other records the total of the two dice when they are multiplied together.

Firstly, find the measures of average for the raw data.

Then team up three pairs of students to combine their data into a frequency distribution. Once the frequency distribution is complete, students should find the measures of average for the combined distribution. Which of these measures is the same as the respective average of the individual measures for the three pairs of students?

Learn 6.2

5 Ask: What does the accuracy of the estimate of the mean for grouped data depend upon?

Give examples of some raw data which when grouped would lead to a good estimate being obtained from the use of midpoints, and some which would not.

Answer: for the midpoints to provide a good estimate, the data needs to be fairly evenly spread around the midpoint. So, for a situation where the data is not evenly spread around the midpoint, for example if all the data values happen to fall in the first half of the class interval into which the data values were placed, then the estimate of the mean could be poor.

Example: for data that was going to be grouped in $10 \leqslant t < 20$, $20 \leqslant t < 30$ and so on.

Data where the estimate would be fairly accurate: 24, 18, 12, 22, 28, 37, 32, 34, 17, 15, 24, 33, 37, 24, 19, 22, 11, 36, 41, 47

Data where the estimate might not be so accurate: 32, 21, 15, 11, 20, 16, 13, 14, 22, 24, 31, 30, 20, 24, 16, 32, 14, 25, 41, 35

Learn... 6.1 **Frequency distributions**

A frequency distribution shows how often individual values occur (the frequency).

The information is usually shown in a frequency table.

A frequency table shows the values and their frequency.

Frequency distributions are usually used with **discrete data**.

Discrete data are data that can only take individual values.

For example, the number of cars is discrete data. You cannot have 2.3 cars!

This frequency table shows the number of pets for students at a school.

There are 5 students with no pets, 11 students with 1 pet, 8 students with 2 pets, ... and so on. You can use the frequency table to calculate measures of average and measures of spread.

Number of pets (x)	Frequency (f)
0	5
1	11
2	8
3	5
4	2

Example:

Here is an additional example showing the number of cats in the houses of 39 students.

There are 21 students with no cats, 10 students with 1 cat, 5 students with 2 cats, and so on. You can use the frequency table to calculate measures of average and measures of spread.

For the frequency distribution above, find:

a the average

b the spread.

Number of cats (x)	Frequency (f)
0	21
1	10
2	5
3	2
4	1

Solution:

a The most common measures of **average** are the **mean**, the **mode** and the **median**.

In an examination, students should choose the most appropriate measure, if they are not guided. For the purposes of this example, all three options are worked through here.

Mean

The mean is the total of all the values divided by the number of values.

The mean here is the total number of pets divided by the total number of students.

$$\text{Mean} = \frac{\text{the total of (frequencies} \times \text{values)}}{\text{the total of frequencies}} = \frac{\Sigma fx}{\Sigma f}$$

where Σ means 'the sum of'.

Number of cats, (x)	Frequency, (f)	Frequency × number of cats (fx)
0	21	$0 \times 21 = 0$
1	10	$1 \times 10 = 10$
2	5	$2 \times 5 = 10$
3	2	$3 \times 2 = 6$
4	1	$4 \times 1 = 4$
	$\Sigma f = 21 + 10 + 5 + 2 + 1 = 39$	$\Sigma fx = 0 + 10 + 10 + 6 + 4 = 30$

$$\text{Mean} = \frac{\text{the total of (frequencies} \times \text{values)}}{\text{the total of frequencies}} = \frac{\Sigma fx}{\Sigma f}$$

$$= \frac{30}{39}$$

$$= 0.76923\ldots$$

$$= 0.77 \text{ (to two d.p.)}$$

The mean is a useful measure of average.

Mode

The mode is the value that has the highest frequency next to it (i.e. the value occurring most often).

'Number of pets is 0' has a frequency of 21 and all the other frequencies are less than this.

Mode = 0

The mode is the number that occurs most frequently.

Median

The median is the middle value when the data are listed in order.

It does not matter whether you go from smallest to highest or the other way round.

The data have 39 values so the median is the $(\frac{39+1}{2})$th value = 20th value.

The data are already ordered in the table.

The first 21 values are 0, the next 10 are 1, so the 20th value is 0

0 0 0 0 0 0 0 0 0 0 0 0 0 0 0 0 0 0 0 0 0 1 1 1 1 1 1 1 …

Median = 0   20th

The median is the middle value when the data are arranged in order.

The median can also be found using the 'running totals' of the frequencies as follows.

Number of cats (x)	Frequency (f)	Running total
0	21	21
1	10	21 + 10 = 31
2	5	21 + 10 + 5 = 36
3	2	21 + 10 + 5 + 2 = 38
4	1	21 + 10 + 5 + 2 + 1 = 39

The 20th value will lie here so the median is 0

b The most common measures of spread are the **range** and the **inter-quartile range**.

Range

The range is the difference between the highest value and the lowest value.

The range = 4 − 0 = 4

Range = 4

The range is a measure of how spread out the data are.

Inter-quartile range

The inter-quartile range is the difference between the upper quartile and the lower quartile.

The lowest quartile is the $\frac{1}{4}(n+1)$th value = $\frac{1}{4}(39+1)$th value = 10th value.

The upper quartile is the $\frac{3}{4}(n+1)$th value = $\frac{3}{4}(39+1)$th value = 30th value.

The quartiles can be found using the same method as the median or else you can consider the 'running totals' of the frequencies as follows.

Number of cats (x)	Frequency (f)	Running total
0	21	21
1	10	21 + 10 = 31
2	5	21 + 10 + 5 = 36
3	2	21 + 10 + 5 + 2 = 38
4	1	21 + 10 + 5 + 2 + 1 = 39

The 10th value will lie here so the lower quartile is 0

The 30th value will lie here so the upper quartile is 1

The inter-quartile range = 1 − 0 = 1

The inter-quartile range is a measure of how spread out the data are. It focuses on the middle 50 per cent of the distribution and is not affected by extreme values.

Teacher notes

In examinations, students do not perform very well when using frequency distributions. Sometimes when finding the mean, some students are good at working with midpoints for continuous frequency distributions but then seem fazed by a discrete frequency distribution where midpoints are not needed.

Knowledge and use of Σfx and Σf will help many students to manage these types of questions successfully.

The introductory example is deliberately unspecific about the measures required. It is important to see the different way that these measures are now tested in examinations. It is likely that students will have to choose appropriate methods of average to work out for a set of data or to compare two sets of data.

Comparison of two sets of data at Higher tier is expected to include one measure of average (from mean, mode and median, perhaps with a reason for choosing one over the other) and the range or the inter-quartile range as a measure of spread.

Number questions relevant to the specification for Unit 1 can be asked about statistical distributions. Therefore, this is included in the Practise exercise in fraction and percentage work.

Problem-solving opportunities and choice of measures for comparison are also possible here, making this work potentially quite demanding.

Common errors

✗ Mixing up the three measures of average.

✗ Forgetting to order values when finding the median.

✗ Leaving the answer for the range and inter-quartile range not calculated, for example 3 − 21 instead of 18.

AQA Examiner's tip

When working out the mean, students often round their answer up to a whole number without showing their working – this could leave an incorrect answer as the only evidence for the question, which would not score any marks. Students should be reminded to show all their working at all times.

Bump up your grade

To get a Grade C, students have to be able to work successfully with measures of average on frequency distributions.

Learn... 6.2 Grouped frequency distributions

A grouped frequency distribution shows how often **grouped data** values occur (the frequency).

The information is usually shown in a grouped frequency table.

A grouped frequency table shows the values and their frequency.

Grouped frequency distributions are usually used with **continuous data**.

Continuous data are data which can take any numerical value. Length and weight are common examples of continuous data.

Discrete data can only take individual values. Shoe sizes are an example.

You can use the grouped frequency table to calculate measures of average and measures of spread as before.

Mean

The mean is the total of all the values divided by the number of values.

$$\text{Mean} = \frac{\text{the total of (frequencies} \times \text{values)}}{\text{the total of frequencies}} = \frac{\Sigma fx}{\Sigma f}$$

where Σ means 'the sum of'.

As the data are grouped, you will need to use the midpoint of each group to represent the value.

Discrete data	Continuous data
To find the midpoint, add together the largest and smallest value of each group and divide the answer by two.	To find the midpoint, add together the smallest possible value (lower bound) and the largest possible value (upper bound) for each group and divide the answer by two.

Mode

The mode is the value which has the highest frequency next to it (i.e. the value occurring most often).

For grouped data it is more usual to find the **modal class**.

The modal class is the class with the highest frequency.

Median

The median is the middle value when the data are listed in order.

For grouped data it is more usual to find the group containing the median.

Graphical work (see Chapter 7) is often used to estimate the median.

Range

The range is the highest value take away the lowest value.

For grouped data it is not always possible to identify the highest value and the lowest value. However, it can be estimated as: highest value in highest group − lowest value in lowest group.

Inter-quartile range

The inter-quartile range is the difference between the upper quartile and the lower quartile.

For grouped data it is not always possible to identify the upper quartile and the lower quartile.

Graphical work (see Chapter 7) is often used to estimate the quartiles.

Example: The table shows the age of children in a hotel during August.

Age, x (years)	Frequency
$0 \leqslant x < 4$	45
$4 \leqslant x < 8$	120
$8 \leqslant x < 12$	208
$12 \leqslant x < 16$	77

$4 \leqslant x < 8$ covers all the values between 4 and 8 years old. The 4 is included in the group whereas the 8 will be in the $8 \leqslant x < 12$ group. The range of values is called a class interval.

Use the information in the grouped frequency table to:

a write down the modal class

b work out the class which contains the median

c calculate an estimate of the mean age of the children in the hotel.

Solution: **a** The modal class is the class with the highest frequency.

This is the class $8 \leqslant x < 12$ (as there are 208 children in this class)

b The median is the middle value when the data are listed in order.

There are 450 values in total so in this case the median is the 225th value.

Age, x (years)	Frequency	Running total
$0 \leqslant x < 4$	45	45
$4 \leqslant x < 8$	120	165 (45 + 120)
$8 \leqslant x < 12$	208	373 (45 + 120 + 208)
$12 \leqslant x < 16$	77	450 (45 + 120 + 208 + 77)

The 225th value will lie in this interval so the median lies in the $8 \leqslant x < 12$ class.

The $8 \leqslant x < 12$ class contains the median.

c The mean is the total of all the values divided by the number of values.

$$\text{Mean} = \frac{\text{the total of (frequencies} \times \text{values)}}{\text{the total of frequencies}} = \frac{\Sigma fx}{\Sigma f}$$

where Σ means 'the sum of'.

As the data are grouped, you will need to use the midpoint of each group.

An additional column should be added to the table for the midpoints.

Age, x (years)	Frequency (f)	Midpoint, x	Frequency × midpoint (fx)
$0 \leqslant x < 4$	45	2	45 × 2 = 90
$4 \leqslant x < 8$	120	6	120 × 6 = 720
$8 \leqslant x < 12$	208	10	208 × 10 = 2080
$12 \leqslant x < 16$	77	14	77 × 14 = 1078
	$\Sigma f = 450$		$\Sigma fx = 3968$

$$\text{Mean} = \frac{\text{the total of (frequencies} \times \text{values)}}{\text{the total of frequencies}} = \frac{\Sigma fx}{\Sigma f}$$

$$= \frac{3968}{450}$$

$$= 8.81777\ldots$$

$$= 8.82 \text{ (to 2 d.p.)}$$

Teacher notes

Students do not always perform well on questions involving grouped frequency distributions. Some use class boundaries instead of midpoints and some divide by the number of groups rather than the total frequency.

The best way to encourage understanding of these types of questions is for students to be asked to stop and think about what the frequency table is telling them – they are then far more likely to use appropriate methods for the averages rather than relying on mechanical methods.

Another issue worthy of discussion is the reason why the mean calculation can only ever provide an estimate. So if raw data is available it is better to use it to calculate exact values of the mean before grouping the data, perhaps for display in a graph.

Using the inter-quartile range can be difficult for grouped data, and graphical methods as illustrated in Chapter 7 are usually the best method to obtain the necessary estimates of the lower and upper quartiles. This then allows an estimate of the inter-quartile range to be worked out.

 Common errors

✗ Failing to consider midpoints.

✗ Failing to identify correct midpoints.

✗ Dividing by the number of groups instead of the total frequency for the calculation of the mean.

AQA **Examiner's tip**

Students need to remember to check that the answer they have obtained is sensible for the data.

The answer must lie within the range of the data.

7 Representing data

Objectives

7.1 Stem-and-leaf diagrams	Specification
D • construct and interpret an ordered stem-and-leaf diagram	Produce charts and diagrams for various graph types … stem-and-leaf diagrams. **S3.2h**
	Interpret a wide range of graphs and diagrams and draw conclusions. **S4.1**

7.2 Line graphs and frequency polygons	Specification
D • construct and interpret line graphs	Interpret a wide range of graphs and diagrams and draw conclusions. **S4.1**
C • construct a frequency polygon	Produce charts and diagrams for various graph types … frequency polygons. **S3.2h**
	Interpret a wide range of graphs and diagrams and draw conclusions. **S4.1**

7.3 Cumulative frequency diagrams	Specification
B • construct and interpret a cumulative frequency diagram for continuous or grouped data	Produce charts and diagrams for various data types: cumulative frequency diagrams. **S3.2h**
• use a cumulative frequency diagram to estimate median and inter-quartile range	Interpret a wide range of graphs and diagrams and draw conclusions. **S4.1**

7.4 Box plots	Specification
B • construct and interpret a box plot	Produce charts and diagrams for various data types: box plots. **S3.2h**
• compare two sets of data using a box plot referencing average and spread	Interpret a wide range of graphs and diagrams and draw conclusions. **S4.1**
	Compare distributions and make inferences. **S4.4**

7.5 Histograms	Specification
D • construct a histogram with equal class intervals	Interpret a wide range of graphs and diagrams and draw conclusions. **S4.1**
A • construct a histogram with unequal class intervals	Produce charts and diagrams for various data types: histograms with unequal class intervals. **S3.2h**
A* • interpret a histogram with unequal class intervals	Interpret a wide range of graphs and diagrams and draw conclusions. **S4.1**

kerboodle! resources

k! Learning activity: Representing data

k! Essential skills: Drawing a cumulative frequency diagram

k! Interactive activity: Box plots

k! Learn: Histograms

k! Worksheet: Representing data 1

k! Worksheet: Representing data 2

k! Test yourself: Representing data

k! On your marks…: Representing data

Starter activities

Learn 7.1   **1**   Many students will have already met stem-and-leaf diagrams but this does not mean they will know all the essential features of these diagrams.

As a means of determining prior knowledge, which could then merge into the main part of the lesson, ask students to identify five features of stem-and-leaf diagrams.

Answer: (five of many possible features) stem usually first digit of data values/leaves usually last digit of data values/stem in numerical order/leaves ordered left to right/must have a key

Learn 7.2

2 Collect examples of graphs from the media (newspapers are usually best but the internet is also a possibility). Ask students to look out for issues that they think make the graphs either difficult to interpret, or perhaps designed to mislead the reader, or give a false impression. Line graphs are usually the most common examples seen.

This idea could be introduced as a starter and discussed as a starter or a plenary in a future lesson.

Learn 7.2

3 Frequency polygons rely on students plotting the points on midpoints of class intervals.

Use this starter to practice finding the midpoint for some different class intervals.

a 15 up to 20   **b** $20 \leqslant t < 30$ **c** $140 < t \leqslant 50$

Answers:

a *17*   **b** *25*   **c** *45*

Learn 7.3

4 Cumulative frequencies must always be plotted against the upper-class boundaries for grouped data. Use some of the grouped frequency distributions from student book Chapter 6 (estimating the mean from a grouped frequency distribution) to help students practise correct identification of upper-class bounds.

Learn 7.4

5 Recap how to find the lower quartile, median and upper quartile for a cumulative frequency distribution. This will be very helpful for this Learn's work on box plots. Ask: How could you make a judgement about the maximum and minimum value of a distribution from a cumulative frequency graph?

Learn 7.5

6 Draw a histogram for a distribution with unequal width classes **incorrectly** by simply drawing bars to the frequency instead of using frequency density. Discuss with the class how this gives an unfair impression of the spread and distribution of the data. In examinations, many students make this mistake and this demonstration may make frequency density more memorable.

An example of such a graph is given here.

The frequency distribution is:

Class width	Frequency
$0 < x \leqslant 20$	8
$20 < x \leqslant 30$	6
$30 < x \leqslant 40$	7
$40 < x \leqslant 50$	4
$50 < x \leqslant 80$	3

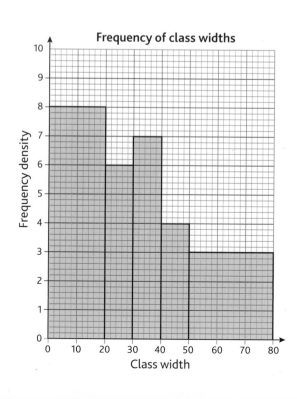

Frequency of class widths

Plenary activities

Learn 7.1 **1** On pieces of card (or display on interactive whiteboard), write down the most important features of a stem-and-leaf diagram together with some features of other diagrams such as pie charts or bar charts. Then ask students to match each feature with its correct diagram.

Learn 7.1 **2** As a means of emphasising the importance of the key in a stem-and-leaf diagram, give the students some examples of a key and ask them what it could actually stand for.

For example, 2 | 8 could mean 28, 2.8, 2 minutes 8 seconds, etc.

What about 3 | 7 or 5 | 13?

Learn 7.1 **3** Explain that a stem-and-leaf diagram should always be ordered in an examination.

However, do students know what features of the data are shown on both an unordered stem-and-leaf diagram and an ordered stem-and-leaf diagram?

What aspects are shown on an ordered stem-and-leaf diagram that cannot be seen on an unordered diagram?

Answer: Both show the distribution of the data, only the ordered one can be used to obtain measures from.

Learn 7.2 **4** One of the starters for 7.2 suggests that students bring in examples from the media of poor or deliberately misleading representations.

For this plenary, students take one of these and draw it accurately, eliminating the issue(s) that have been highlighted as making it inappropriate.

Learn 7.3–7.5 **5** As has been discussed, a key skill required by students is the ability to make an appropriate choice of diagram when prompted.

Give students a variety of data sets and a list of the diagrams they have learned about.

Ask them to choose the type of diagram they would use to represent each data set with reasons for their choice.

Discuss their answers.

(This is potentially worthy of a full lesson where they actually then go ahead and draw their choice of diagram for the set(s) of data.)

Learn 7.3–7.5 **6** Students collect information from their work/school/family about any of the following areas:

- height
- arm length
- head circumference
- running time over a fixed distance
- pulse rate
- heart rate
- time taken to complete homework
- time taken to travel to work/school
- time spent sleeping/eating/exercising.

They use this information to create their own personal cumulative frequency diagram/box plot/histogram and find out where they lie on the distribution.

Learn... 7.1 Stem-and-leaf diagrams

Stem-and-leaf diagrams are a useful way of representing data.

They are used to show discrete data, or continuous data that has been rounded.

Stem-and-leaf diagrams need a key to show the 'stem' and 'leaf'.

For two-digit numbers the first digit is the stem and the second digit is the leaf.

It is often useful to provide an ordered stem-and-leaf diagram where the items are placed in order.

1	1 6 7 8 9
2	2 2 7 7 7 8 9
3	1 4 6

Key 3|1 represents 31

If the numbers are decimals such as 5.4, the stem would be the 5 and the leaves would represent the decimal parts.

Example: The results below represent the times of the 24 competitors in a 100 m competition. Three races, each of eight people, took place with the fastest eight people overall qualifying for the final.

The times were, in seconds to two decimal places (d.p.).

10.12	10.25	10.05	10.62	10.45	10.39
10.02	9.99	10.35	10.30	10.19	10.27
10.31	10.20	9.96	10.52	10.38	10.11
10.32	10.04	10.18	10.44	10.22	10.23

a Draw an ordered stem-and-leaf diagram for these results.

b Find the median time.

c Write down the eight times of the people who qualified for the final.

Solution: **a** As all the data starts with 9 or 10, using the integers as the stem would only give two rows.

Instead, use 9.9 up to 10.6 as the stem and the final (second decimal place) value as the leaves.

For example, 10.12 is a leaf of 2 on the 10.1 row, 10.25 is a leaf of 5 on the 10.2 row and so on.

Firstly, complete the unordered diagram.

Times for competitors

9.9	9 6
10.0	5 2 4
10.1	2 9 1 8
10.2	5 7 0 2 3
10.3	9 5 0 1 8 2
10.4	5 4
10.5	2
10.6	2

Key 9.9 | 6 represents 9.96 seconds

Now the leaves are written in order to give an ordered stem-and-leaf diagram.

Remember to include a key.

Times for competitors

9.9	6	9			
10.0	2	4	5		
10.1	1	2	8	9	
10.2	0	2	3	5	7
10.3	0	1	2	5	8	9
10.4	4	5			
10.5	2				
10.6	2				

Key 9.9 | 6 represents 9.96 seconds

b As there are 24 values, the median is halfway between the 12th and 13th values.

Count up the ordered stem and leaf to find these values.

12th value = 10.23

13th value = 10.25

Therefore the median is 10.24 seconds (halfway between the two values)

c The fastest eight students qualified for the final.

These times were 9.96, 9.99, 10.02, 10.04, 10.05, 10.11, 10.12 and 10.18 seconds.

Teacher notes

It is good practice to explain to students what type of data these diagrams are for. Students should always be encouraged to complete an unordered stem-and-leaf diagram first before ordering takes place, otherwise errors are inevitable.

In examinations, there is often a mark for completing a key and this mark is often neglected by students despite clear reminders in the question writing.

Common errors

✗ Forgetting to put a key in a stem-and-leaf diagram if one is not provided, or misinterpreting the key given.

✗ Reversing the order of the left-hand data in back-to-back diagrams.

✗ Missing out one of the values – students should always check that the number of leaves is equal to the number of data values.

AQA Examiner's tip

Students should always complete an unordered stem-and-leaf diagram first. It is then far easier to complete the ordered one. There will always be space to do this on the exam paper.

Bump up your grade

To get a Grade C, students should remember to write a key on their stem-and-leaf diagrams.

Learn... 7.2 Line graphs and frequency polygons

Line graphs

A **line graph** is a series of points joined with straight lines.

Line graphs show how data change over a period of time.

Example: The table shows the heart rate (beats per minute) of a student after exercise.

Time (minutes)	0	1	2	3	4	5	6	7
Heart rate (bpm)	141	145	119	87	73	67	64	64

    a Draw a line graph to show this information.

    b Use your line graph to estimate the time at which the rate returned to below 100 bpm.

Solution: **a**

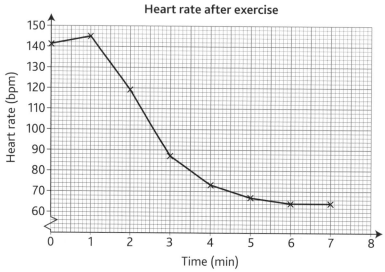

    b Reading across from 100 on the vertical axis, you can estimate this time to be about 2.6 minutes (2 minutes 36 seconds, as 0.6 of a minute is 0.6 × 60 = 36 seconds).

Frequency polygons

A **frequency polygon** is a way of showing continuous grouped data in a diagram.

Points are plotted at the midpoint of each class interval.

For a frequency polygon, the groups may have equal or unequal widths.

The frequency polygon is an example of a **frequency diagram**.

Another type of frequency diagram is a **histogram**.

Histograms are discussed in Learn 7.5.

Example: The data shows the time, to the nearest hour, taken for a group of pigeons to return to their loft after being released.

Draw a frequency polygon for these data.

Time, t (hours)	Frequency
$1 < t \leqslant 5$	13
$5 < t \leqslant 9$	67
$9 < t \leqslant 13$	22
$13 < t \leqslant 17$	7
$17 < t \leqslant 20$	3

Solution: For a frequency polygon, points are plotted at the midpoint of each class at the correct frequency.

e.g. the midpoint for $1 < t \leqslant 5$ is $\dfrac{1+5}{2} = 3$

and so on.

Points are joined with straight lines.

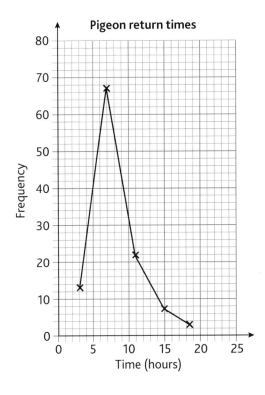

Teacher notes

Line graphs will usually be representations of data occurring over a period of time. However, though these are really time series, that term is not used in this specification. It is important that students know when they should use joined up line graphs for, for example, quantitative data or discrete data, where the lines between the points can have no meaning.

 Common errors

✗ Labelling frequency diagrams with the class intervals rather than a continuous scale.

✗ Drawing the frequency polygon **and** a histogram on the same axes when only one has been asked for.

✗ Plotting points incorrectly – more care is needed, particularly in reading scales.

AQA Examiner's tip

Students should not label the horizontal axis with the class intervals.

There is also no need for students to draw the frequency polygon before and beyond the first and last plotted point.

Bump up your grade

To get a Grade C, students need to be capable of accurately plotting points at correct midpoints for a frequency polygon.

 Learn... **7.3 Cumulative frequency diagrams**

A **cumulative frequency diagram** (or cumulative frequency curve) is used to estimate the median and quartiles of a set of data.

To find the **cumulative frequency**, you add the frequencies in turn to give you a 'running total'.

Cumulative frequencies are plotted at the upper class bound. The upper class bound is the highest possible value for each class interval.

The cumulative frequency diagram is formed by joining the points with a series of straight lines or a smooth curve.

The total cumulative frequency can be divided by four to find the quartiles and the median. This is shown in the alternative example that follows the Teacher notes.

Teacher notes

Finding the upper class bound is shown in the example for one type of labelling. Other ways of labelling groups are:

Height (metres)
$0 < h \leqslant 2$
$2 < h \leqslant 4$
$4 < h \leqslant 8$
$8 < h \leqslant 12$

In this case, the label $2 < h \leqslant 4$ means greater than 2 and less than or equal to 4. The value of 4 metres will be included in this interval.

The cumulative frequency plots will be at 2, 4, 8 and 12.

Height (metres)
0–
2–
4–
8–12

In this case, the label 2– means greater than or equal to 2 and less than 4. The value of 4 metres will be included in the following interval. Only the last interval has a closing value, that is, 12.

The cumulative frequency plots will be at 2, 4, 8 and 12.

Height (metres)
0 up to 2
2 up to 4
4 up to 8
8 up to 12

This method of labelling covers the full range, so that '2 up to 4' includes all the values from 2 to 4 except 4. The value 4 will be included in the '4 up to 8' interval.

The cumulative frequency plots will be at 2, 4, 8 and 12.

Height (metres)
1–2
3–4
5–8
9–12

In this case, the measurements are to the nearest metre, so that the 1–2 interval will stretch from 0.5 to 2.5 (that is, a class width of 2). Similarly, the 9–12 interval will stretch from 8.5 to 12.5 (that is, a class width of 4).

The cumulative frequency plots will be at 2.5, 4.5, 8.5 and 12.5.

The cumulative frequency can be divided by four to find the quartiles and the median as follows:

- The lower quartile is one quarter along the cumulative frequency.
- The median is one half along the cumulative frequency.
- The upper quartile is three quarters along the cumulative frequency.

The example shows this being completed.

Example: The waiting times at a dentist are recorded in the table below.

Time, t (min)	Frequency
$0 \leqslant t < 5$	8
$5 \leqslant t < 10$	12
$10 \leqslant t < 15$	7
$15 \leqslant t < 30$	3

a Show this information on a cumulative frequency diagram.

b Use your cumulative frequency diagram to estimate:

  i   the median

  ii the inter-quartile range

  iii the percentage of people waiting over 20 minutes.

Solution: **a** It is useful to add an extra column to the table.

    This can be used to show the cumulative frequencies.

Time (min)	Frequency	Cumulative frequency
$0 \leqslant t < 5$	8	8
$5 \leqslant t < 10$	12	8 + 12 = 20
$10 \leqslant t < 15$	7	8 + 12 + 7 = 27
$15 \leqslant t < 30$	3	8 + 12 + 7 + 3 = 30

Now plot these cumulative frequencies at the upper class boundaries.

The upper class bounds for each interval are 5, 10, 15 and 30 respectively.

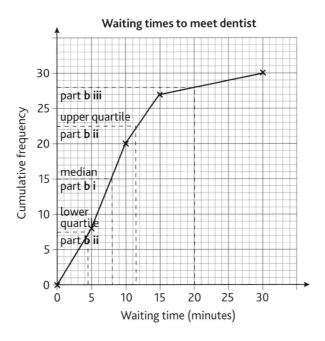

b i   The median is read off at the halfway point in the whole of the data set.

There are 30 values, so the median is the $\frac{1}{2} \times$ 30th value = 15th value.

From the graph, median = 8 minutes. (Note that the median is the $\frac{(n+1)}{2}$ th value, which is $\frac{31}{2} = 15.5$ but when n is large it is simpler to just halve the cumulative frequency. The difference in outcome is negligible. This idea is also used in the position of the quartiles.)

ii   To estimate the inter-quartile range, first you need to estimate the lower and upper quartiles.

The lower quartile is read off at the point one quarter along the data.

There are 30 values, so the lower quartile is the $\frac{1}{4} \times$ 30th value = 7.5th value.

From the graph, lower quartile = 4.5 minutes.

The upper quartile is read off at the point three quarters along the data.

There are 30 values, so the upper quartile is the $\frac{3}{4} \times$ 30th = 22.5th value.

From the graph, upper quartile = 11.5 minutes.

The inter-quartile range = upper quartile – lower quartile

$$= 11.5 - 4.5$$

$$= 7 \text{ minutes}$$

(This means there is a 7 minute range across the middle 50% of the data.)

iii To find an estimate of the percentage of waiting times over 20 minutes.

Draw a line from 20 minutes on the horizontal axis to the cumulative frequency graph.

From the graph, this reading = 28 people waiting.

There are 28 people waiting **below** 20 minutes.

There are 30 − 28 = 2 people waiting **above** 20 minutes.

This represents $\frac{2}{30}$ calls = $\frac{2}{30} \times 100\%$ = 6.67%

Teacher notes

Cumulative frequency is often answered well by students, but many fail to plot at the upper class boundaries. Students are free to draw either a curve or a polygon in examination questions. However, it is often much easier if students use a ruler to draw a polygon. This is because invariably they will draw untidy curves, which may lose credit if, for example, they miss some of the points.

When finding medians by estimation on a cumulative frequency curve, the value along the data can be found by either dividing the total frequency by 2, or by adding 1 and then dividing by 2. As the value is an estimate, either is perfectly acceptable. The position of the lower quartile and upper quartile can be dealt with in a similar way.

Common errors

✗ Plotting at midpoints instead of upper class bounds.

✗ Plotting frequencies instead of cumulative frequencies.

✗ Mistaking the *position* of the median, lower quartile and upper quartile as the actual value of the median, lower quartile or upper quartile.

✗ Scaling issues – students must check the value of one small square on both axes.

AQA Examiner's tip

Students should take care to check the total cumulative frequency when halving to find the position of the median. It is not always the highest label on the graph.

Learn... 7.4 Box plots

A box plot (sometimes called a box-and-whisker diagram) is another way to show information about a frequency distribution.

The box plot provides a visual summary of information.

It can be used to compare two or more distributions.

The box plot shows the following information:

- the minimum and maximum values
- the lower and upper quartiles
- the median.

Example: The data for the dentist waiting times are given again below.

Time (min)	Frequency
$0 \leqslant t < 5$	8
$5 \leqslant t < 10$	12
$10 \leqslant t < 15$	7
$15 \leqslant t < 30$	3

Draw a box plot for the data.

Solution: From the example in the previous Learn, the following estimates were obtained.

Lower quartile = 4.5

Median = 8

Upper quartile = 11.5

You do not know the minimum and maximum values but looking at the class intervals you can best estimate the minimum value as 0 and the maximum value as 30. (You have no additional information so cannot really assume otherwise.)

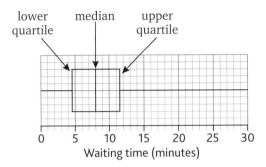

Waiting time (minutes)

Teacher notes

Box plots do not require work regarding the plotting of outliers in GCSE Mathematics. However, any outliers present in data should always be considered by students for the validity of data and in comparing different sets. If outliers do occur, it is acceptable for the whiskers to run all the way to the outliers.

Outliers are values which seem to be a long way away from the rest of the data, so using them in calculations and diagrams can tend to cause the results to be very different to what they would be if that single value was not present.

Students should be aware of the usefulness of box plots when comparing two sets of data, as the medians (measure of average) and the interquartile range and the range (two measures of spread) are clearly visible from the plots.

At Higher tier it is usual to use the interquartile range rather than the range as the former is not affected by possible outliers. This is because the bottom 25% of the data (below the lower quartile) and the top 25% of the data (above the upper quartile) are not used when considering the interquartile range.

Common errors

✗ Scaling issues – students must check the value for each small square on the scale.

✗ Failing to draw a numbered and labelled scale for the box plot.

✗ Joining the whiskers to make another box.

AQA Examiner's tip

Box plots can be achieved by dropping lines down from the appropriate position on the cumulative frequency graph as illustrated in the Student Book. However, in examination questions it is possible there might not be room on the paper to do this. Consequently, students should not rely on this method.

Learn... 7.5 Histograms

Histograms

A histogram is a way of showing continuous grouped data in a diagram.

The area of the bar represents the frequency.

For a histogram, the groups may have equal or unequal widths.

The histogram is an example of a frequency diagram.

Another type of frequency diagram is a frequency polygon.

Frequency polygons were discussed in Learn 7.2 Line graphs and frequency polygons.

Histograms with equal group widths

In a histogram, the area of the bars represents the frequency.

If the group widths are equal, bars are drawn to the height of the frequency.

Example: The data shows the time, to the nearest hour, taken for a group of pigeons to return to their loft after being released.

Time, t (hours)	Frequency
$1 \leqslant t < 5$	13
$5 \leqslant t < 9$	67
$9 \leqslant t < 13$	22
$13 \leqslant t < 17$	7
$17 \leqslant t < 21$	3

Draw a histogram to represent these data.

Solution: As the classes are of equal widths, the bars can simply be drawn to the heights of the frequencies. There must be no gaps between bars.

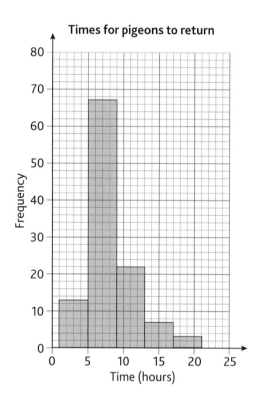

Histograms with unequal group widths

For a histogram, the groups may have equal or unequal widths.

In a histogram, the area of the bars represents the frequency.

If the group widths are unequal, bars are drawn to the height of the frequency density.

$$\text{Frequency density} = \frac{\text{frequency}}{\text{class width}}$$

Example: The total bill for each of the couples eating in a restaurant one evening is shown in the table.

Draw a histogram for the data.

Bill, p (pounds)	Frequency
$10 \leqslant p < 20$	5
$20 \leqslant p < 30$	22
$30 \leqslant p < 35$	18
$35 \leqslant p < 50$	30
$50 \leqslant p < 100$	12

Solution: Use a continuous scale for the *x*-axis.

As the groups are unequal width, bars are drawn to the height of the frequency density.

$$\textbf{Frequency density} = \frac{\textbf{frequency}}{\textbf{class width}}$$

It is useful to add two extra columns to the table.

One column can be used to show the class width.

The other column can be used to show the frequency density.

Bill, p (pounds)	Frequency	Class width	Frequency density $(= \frac{\text{frequency}}{\text{class width}})$
$10 \leqslant p < 20$	5	10	$5 \div 10 = 0.5$
$20 \leqslant p < 30$	22	10	$22 \div 10 = 2.2$
$30 \leqslant p < 35$	18	5	$18 \div 5 = 3.6$
$35 \leqslant p < 50$	30	15	$30 \div 15 = 2$
$50 \leqslant p < 100$	12	50	$12 \div 50 = 0.24$

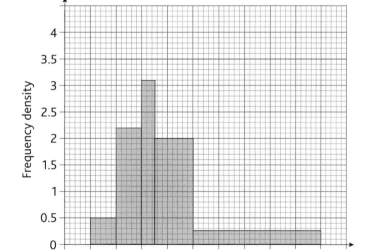

Total bill in a restaurant

The bars can simply be drawn to the limits of the class interval labels to ensure that there are no gaps in the diagram.

Teacher notes

Histograms may or may not have equal class widths. For unequal class widths, the use of frequency density is the expected method for GCSE Mathematics. It is possible to use a method of a number of squares counting for a particular number of items and then using a key but students using frequency density tend to be more successful.

Many students make mistakes by drawing their histograms like bar charts with gaps in them. Others draw unequal class width histograms like their equal class width histograms with no frequency density calculations.

If students are guided in an examination question to draw a 'suitable' or 'appropriate' diagram, then a frequency polygon or histogram are suitable for equal class width data. For unequal class width data, a histogram would be expected.

Common errors

✗ Leaving gaps between bars.

✗ Not calculating frequency density for unequal class width histograms.

✗ Dividing class width by frequency instead of the correct way around.

✗ Reading scales incorrectly – remind students to check the value of one small square.

AQA Examiner's tip

Students may be asked to draw a frequency diagram. They would then have a choice of drawing a histogram or a frequency polygon.

If the classes are of equal width, it is usually easier to draw a histogram – if students draw a frequency polygon, they will have to the get the midpoints correct.

Scatter graphs

Objectives

1.1 Interpreting scatter graphs		Specification	
D	● draw a scatter graph by plotting points on a graph ● interpret the scatter graph	Produce charts and diagrams for various data types: scatter graphs.	S3.2
C	● identify the type and strength of the correlation	Recognise correlation and draw and/or use lines of best fit by eye, understanding what these represent.	S4.3

8.2 Lines of best fit		Specification	
C	● draw a line of best fit on the scatter graph ● interpret the line of best fit	Recognise correlation and draw and/or use lines of best fit by eye, understanding what these represent.	S4.3

kerboodle! resources

(k!) Matching pairs: Indentifying correlation

(k!) Interactive activity: Correlation and lines of best fit

(k!) Worksheet: Scatter graphs 1

(k!) Worksheet: Scatter graphs 2

(k!) Test yourself: Interpreting scatter graphs
On your marks...: Scatter graphs

Starter activities

Learn 8.1/8.2 **1** Measure height and arm length for students in a class or otherwise set as a task to be undertaken in preparation for a lesson. Plot the information on a graph (for example, class graph). Ask students what they notice.

Learn 8.1/8.2 **2** Discuss how you would collect data to pursue hypotheses such as 'older people get more fractures' or to investigate the relationship between stress and blood pressure and smoking and lung cancer.

Learn 8.2 **3** Practise plotting lines of best fit by eye so that students are required to draw a line on a previously populated scatter graph. How do they ensure that the line is a best fit? What rules to they use? Share this with others in the class.

Learn 8.2 **4** Make use of spreadsheets (and other available software) for plotting scatter graphs and identifying lines of best fit on the diagrams.

Plenary activities

Learn 8.1 **1** Check understanding of correlation by asking questions such as: Write pairs of variables that might show strong positive correlation, strong negative correlation, weak positive correlation, weak negative correlation and no correlation.

Learn 8.1   **2**   Name a variable, for example height, weight, sales of beach balls. Then ask students to name a variable that would show strong/weak, positive/negative or zero correlation when plotted against your variable.

Learn 8.2   **3**   Make up some data sets that might create spurious relationships, for example:
- increase in life expectancy and increase in sales of washing machines (both are related to standard of living)
- increase in the price of milk and increase in the cost of buying a car (both are related to the rise in the cost of living).

Learn 8.2   **4**   Provide (anonymous) statistics for GCSE results and explore possible links. Different groups can be assigned to look at different areas and present a brief report.

Learn 8.2   **5**   Ask students to provide examples of two sets of data that would exhibit:
- perfect correlation (all points in a straight line)
- strong correlation
- weak correlation
- no correlation.

Learn... 8.1   Interpreting scatter graphs

Scatter graphs (or scatter diagrams) are used to show the relationship between two sets of data.

Correlation measures the relationship between two sets of data.

It is measured in terms of **type** and **strength** of correlation.

Type of correlation

Positive correlation	Negative correlation	Zero or no correlation
Positive correlation	**Negative correlation**	**Zero or no correlation**
As one set of data increases, the other set of data increases.	As one set of data increases, the other set of data decreases.	There is no obvious relationship between the two sets of data.

Example:
Temperature against ice-cream sales. As the temperature increases, the number of ice-cream sales increases.

Example:
Temperature against sale of coats. As the temperature increases, the sale of coats decreases.

Example:
Temperature against toothpaste sales. There is no obvious relationship between temperature and toothpaste sales.

Strength of correlation

Strong correlation		Weak correlation
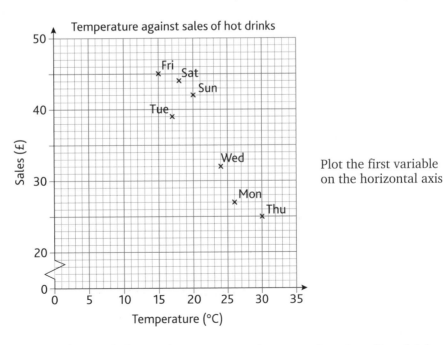		The strength of correlation is a measure of how close the points lie to a straight line (perfect correlation). Watch out for **outliers** (or **rogue values**), which are values that do not fit the data. Correlation is usually measured in terms of strong correlation, weak correlation or no correlation.

Example: A shopkeeper notes the temperature and the number of hot drinks sold each day.

	Sun	Mon	Tue	Wed	Thu	Fri	Sat
Temperature (°C)	20	26	17	24	30	15	18
Hot drink sales	42	27	39	32	25	45	44

Show this information on a scatter graph.

What do you notice from your scatter graph?

Solution: The information can be plotted as a series of coordinate pairs.

	Sun	Mon	Tue	Wed	Thu	Fri	Sat
Temperature (°C)	20	26	17	24	30	15	18
Hot drink sales	42	27	39	32	25	45	44
	(20, 42)	(26, 27)	(17, 39)	(24, 32)	(30, 25)	(15, 45)	(18, 44)

Plot the first variable on the horizontal axis

You can see from the graph that as the temperature increases, the sales of hot drinks decrease.

There is a link between the temperature and hot drink sales.

Teacher notes

It is useful to discuss issues around the scales on graphs and how to choose scales carefully to maximise the size of the graph. Similarly, it might be useful to discuss reading scales and practising identifying the scale on the axes.

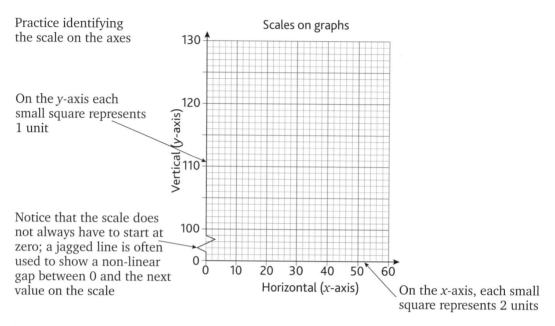

Practice identifying the scale on the axes

Scales on graphs

On the y-axis each small square represents 1 unit

Notice that the scale does not always have to start at zero; a jagged line is often used to show a non-linear gap between 0 and the next value on the scale

On the x-axis, each small square represents 2 units

Remember that correlation measures the relationship between two sets of data. It is measured in terms of type and strength of correlation. For the hot drink sales on the previous page, there is a strong negative correlation.

Discuss with the students what constitutes:

■ perfect correlation (all points in a straight line)

■ strong correlation

■ weak correlation

■ no correlation.

The diagram above may be useful to focus this discussion.

 Common errors

✗ Incorrect use of scale, so not checking what each small square is worth before giving answers.

✗ Plotting coordinates the wrong way around or muddling axes – the independent variable should be on the horizontal axis.

✗ Not identifying and dealing with outliers, which may affect the line of best fit. If students have an outlier, they should always check to make sure they have not made an error.

AQA **Examiner's tip**

Students should be encouraged to use a sharp pencil for their graphical work.

Remind students to label each of their axes and offer a title for the work.

Bump up your grade

Students need to interpret their lines of best fit in terms of the variables, not just describe the relationship in order to get a Grade C.

Learn... 8.2 Lines of best fit

A **line of best fit** is drawn to represent the relationship between two sets of data on a scatter graph.

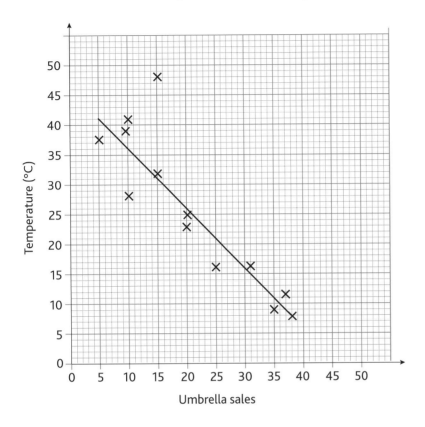

In this example, one of the values does not seem to fit the rest of the dates. This is called an outlier or rogue value. Ignore these values when drawing a line of best fit.

You should draw the line of best fit so that:

- it gives a general trend for all of the data on the scatter graph
- it gives an idea of the strength and type of correlation
- there are roughly equal numbers of points above and below the line.

You can use the line of best fit to estimate missing data.

A line of best fit should only be drawn where the correlation is strong.

Example: Use a line of best fit to estimate the likely sales of hot drinks for a temperature of 22°C.

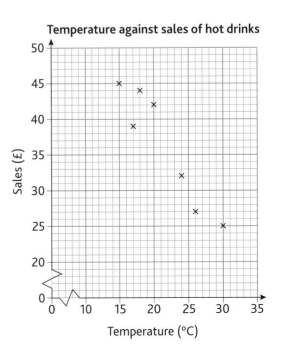

Solution: Drawing the line of best fit on the diagram:

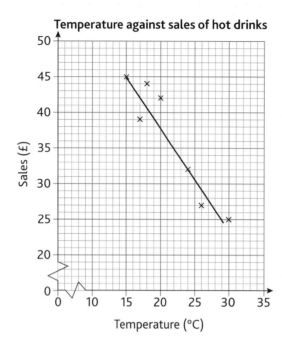

Use the graph to estimate the likely sales of hot drinks for a temperature of 22°C by drawing lines as shown below.

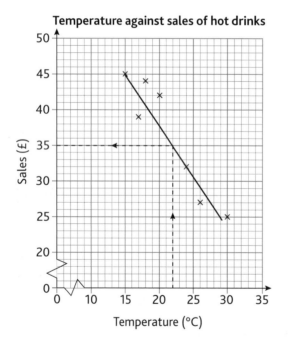

From the graph, the number of hot drinks sales is 35 (34–36 would be acceptable answers as the graph reads 35).

Students might also use a line of best fit to estimate the temperature given the number of hot drink sales – but it is not likely that they would need to do this in real life.

Teacher notes

Students should draw the line of best fit so that:

- it gives a general trend for all of the data on the scatter graph
- it gives an idea of the strength and type of correlation
- roughly equal numbers of points are above and below the line.

For additional accuracy, the line of best fit should pass through the point $(\bar{x}, \bar{y})$ where $\bar{x}$ is the mean of all the x-values and $\bar{y}$ is the mean of all the y-values.

i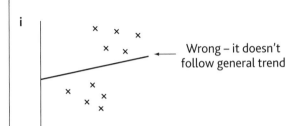

iii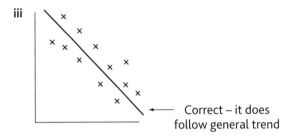

ii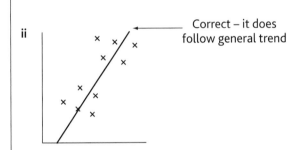

iv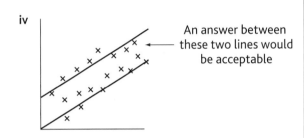

When plotting a line of best fit, there will usually be a 'corridor of success'. This means that if the line of best fit falls between these two lines, it is correct.

For some graphs, a straight line is not possible and a curve of best fit may be appropriate.

 Common errors

✗ Plotting coordinates the wrong way around or confusing axes.

✗ Not dealing with outliers.

✗ Tendency to describe relationships rather than interpret them.

✗ Not appreciating that estimates are most accurate in the middle of the ranges and less accurate at the extremes.

AQA Examiner's tip

The line of best fit does not need to pass through as many points as possible, nor does it have to pass through the origin.

Lines of best fit are marked using a 'corridor of success'. This means that if the line of best fit falls between these two lines, then the line gains full marks.

Bump up your grade

Students need to interpret their lines of best fit in terms of the variables, not just describe the relationship in order to get a Grade C.

 **Probability**

Objectives

9.1 Mutually exclusive events	Specification
D • use a two-way table to find a probability • understand mutually exclusive events • identify different mutually exclusive events and know, if they cover all the possibilities, then the sum of their probabilities is 1	List all outcomes for single events, and for two successive events, in a systematic way and derive related probabilities. **S5.3** Identify different mutually exclusive events and know that the sum of the probabilities of all these events is 1. **S5.4**
9.2 Relative frequency	**Specification**
C • use probability to estimate outcomes for a population • understand and use relative frequency	Understand and use estimates or measures of probability from theoretical models (including equally likely outcomes) or from relative frequency. **S5.2** Understand that increasing sample size generally leads to better estimates of probability and population characteristics. **S5.9** Understand that if an experiment is repeated, this may – and usually will – result in different outcomes. **S5.8**
9.3 Independent events and tree diagrams	**Specification**
B • draw tree diagrams **A** • understand independent and non-independent events • find probabilities of successive independent events	Use tree diagrams to represent outcomes of compound events ... **S5.6h** Use tree diagrams to represent outcomes of compound events, recognising when events are independent. **S5.6h** Know when to add or multiply two probabilities ... if A and B are independent events, the probability of A and B occurring is P(A) × P(B). **S5.5h**
9.4 Dependent events and conditional probability	**Specification**
A* • find probabilities of successive dependent events	Know when to add or multiply two probabilities: if A and B are mutually exclusive, then the probability of A or B occurring is $P(A) + P(B)$, whereas if A and B are independent events, the probability of A and B occurring is $P(A) \times P(B)$. **S5.5h**

kerboodle! resources

- **k!** PowerPoint: Mutually exclusive events
- **k!** Interactive activity: Outcomes
- **k!** 0-9: Combing events
- **k!** Watch out!: Tree diagram
- **k!** PowerPoint: Tree diagrams

- **k!** Worksheet: Probability 1
- **k!** Worksheet: Probability 2
- **k!** Test yourself: Probability
- **k!** On your marks...: Probability

Starter activities

Learn 9.1

1 Explain the contents of a standard pack of cards to students (this will help for later work).

Ask one student to pick a card at random from the pack. Ask:
- What does 'at random' mean in this situation?
- What is the probability that the card is a king?
- What is the probability that the card is a queen?
- What is the probability that the card is a king AND a queen?
- What is the probability that the card is a king OR a queen?

Explain that the events picking a 'king' and 'queen' are mutually exclusive and move into the main part of the lesson. If thought useful, students could also practise accurate use of probability language as well as values.

This could also be an excellent introduction to the issues of addition of probabilities. Students can be shown the 'successful' outcomes each time, which will demonstrate that the probabilities can be added if both events cannot happen at the same time. This could be followed up with additional work showing an example when probabilities cannot be added for example, diamond, 9, diamond and 9, diamond or 9.

Learn 9.1

2 This game may be played in pairs, in groups or as a whole class. Give one student all the cards of one suit from a pack of cards (e.g. ace to king of diamonds). The cards are mixed up and then turned face down in a line. It is important that no one sees what order the cards have been placed in. Without looking at any of the cards, pose some questions to help students think about the probabilities. For example:
- What is the probability of choosing the king?
- What is the probability of choosing the queen?
- What is the probability of choosing the king or the queen?
- What is the probability of choosing a card less than 3?

Ask one of the students to give an outcome that is more likely to happen than not happen.

Now ask one student to turn over the first card.

What is the probability that the next card is higher (or lower)?

Based on probability, what should you choose, higher or lower?

Ask one student, or different students in turn, to always choose the more likely outcome (higher or lower). See whether they can turn over every card in the line without making a mistake. Do students understand why they don't always predict the correct outcome, even if they choose the more likely option?

Learn 9.1

3 The probability of something not happening is 1 minus the probability it does happen.

Consequently, the ability to subtract fractions and decimals from 1 is a useful skill to have for this work, even though the use of a calculator is permitted for this unit.

For a quick fire question and answer starter, ask students to take the following values away from 1:

a 0.3, 0.6, 0.5, 0.1, 0.9, 0.76, 0.54, 0.33, 0.91, 0.04, 0.435, 0.702, 0.987, 0.729, 0.004

b $\frac{1}{2}, \frac{1}{4}, \frac{3}{4}, \frac{4}{7}, \frac{9}{10}, \frac{2}{13}, \frac{7}{8}, \frac{10}{11}, \frac{99}{100}, \frac{17}{25}, \frac{12}{19}, \frac{537}{1000}, \frac{43}{77}, \frac{123}{131}$

Learn 9.2

3 Ask all students to produce a coin. (You may need to keep a supply of pennies!)

What do they think is the probability that the coin lands heads when thrown?

What assumption was made to get that answer?

Each student should now throw the coin twice. Did everyone get heads once and tails once?

Why not?

What about if the coin is thrown 10 times? 20 times? 50 times? 100 times?

Pair students up – one to throw the coin and one to record outcomes on a prepared data collection sheet.

Students work out the proportion of heads after the 10, 20, 50 and 100 tosses (the recorder needs to keep a careful check of the number of throws being done).

What happened to these experimental probabilities (relative frequencies) as the experiment progressed?

Learn 9.2

4 (This starter will take a little preparation but will be worthwhile.)

Fill a large non-transparent bag with a number (e.g. 20) of coloured counters. Make sure you know how many of each colour there are.

Students take it in turn to pick a counter at random from the bag, note the colour and replace the counter in the bag.

Based on each student picking once, students estimate how many of each colour there are in the bag.

Repeat to get more data and a better estimate – this also shows that if an experiment is repeated, outcomes are almost certain to be different.

This starter can be extended to a game for two students where counters are removed **without** replacement. Based on the results of their earlier experiments, can students predict the colour of the next counter drawn until there are none left. Correct prediction could score a point and receive another turn, otherwise the other student gets a turn.

Learn 9.3

5 Look at the experiments and events below and ask students to explain whether they are likely to be independent or not.

Experiment	**Event**
1 Roll a dice	**A** – score a 5 **B** – score a 3
2 Roll a dice and throw a coin	**A** – score a 5 **B** – obtain a head
3 A pair of twin brothers	**A** – first brother is right-handed
	B – second brother is right-handed
4 Weather on 25 June 2012 and 25 December 2012.	**A** – it rains on 25 June
	B – it rains on 25 December
5 Weather on 25 June 2012 and 26 June 2012.	**A** – it rains on 25 June
	B – it rains on 26 June

Answers:

1 Not independent, getting a 5 definitely affects the chance of getting a 3!

2 Independent – outcomes of rolling a dice and throwing a coin cannot possibly affect each other.

3 Not independent – genetics, family traits, upbringing, and so on means there is likely to be a connection between the way the twin brothers use their hands.

4 Independent – the weather on days 6 months apart cannot really be connected.

5 Not independent – weather on consecutive days is not independent, the same weather systems will be around the British Isles on two consecutive days.

Learn 9.4

6 Students try to draw tree diagrams on their mini-whiteboards (structure only not probabilities). This will enable students to focus on the structure only, as many will not know how to draw the diagrams.

Here are two situations:

A – A raffle has 100 tickets numbered 1–100. Tickets ending in 0 win a prize. Alun buys the first ticket and Baz buys the second ticket.

B – A bag contains 10 red and 30 black counters. One counter is taken without replacement and then a second counter is taken.

Learn 9.4

7 Using the tree diagrams from Starter 6, fill in the probabilities on each branch and work out the probability of all possible outcomes.

Answer: (probabilities on the branches should be as given)

A Alan wins = $\frac{10}{100}$ Baz wins = $\frac{9}{99}$ both win = $\frac{90}{9900}$

Alan wins = $\frac{10}{100}$ Baz does not win = $\frac{90}{99}$ Alan wins and Baz does not = $\frac{900}{9900}$

Alan does not win = $\frac{90}{100}$ Baz wins = $\frac{10}{99}$ Alan does not win and Baz wins = $\frac{900}{9900}$

Alan does not win = $\frac{90}{100}$ Baz does not win = $\frac{89}{99}$ both do not win = $\frac{8010}{9900}$

B First red = $\frac{10}{40}$, second red = $\frac{9}{39}$ both red = $\frac{90}{1560}$

First red = $\frac{10}{40}$, second black = $\frac{30}{39}$, red then black = $\frac{300}{1560}$

First black = $\frac{30}{40}$, second red = $\frac{10}{39}$, black then red = $\frac{300}{1560}$

First black = $\frac{30}{40}$, second black = $\frac{29}{39}$, both black = $\frac{870}{1560}$

Plenary activities

Learn 9.1

1 A box contains coloured balls. The balls are coloured blue (B), white (W), red (R) and yellow (Y), as shown in the following diagram.

A ball is taken at random from the box.

The colour is recorded and the ball is put back.

Here are the answers to five questions about this experiment.

Can the students tell you the questions?

a $\frac{7}{24}$ **b** 0.25   **c** 0   **d** evens

e 25 yellows

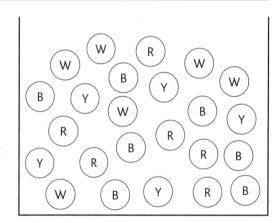

Answers:

a P(blue)?

b P(red) or P(white)?

c P(orange)?

d P(red or white) or P(blue or yellow)?

e How many yellows would you expect if you took a ball and replaced it 120 times?

Learn 9.2

2 Explain that a bag has some counters inside it.

Each counter has a number on it. The number is 0, 1, 2 or 3.

Sam picks a counter out of the bag and notes the number. She then puts it back in the bag and shakes the bag. She then repeats the process until she has taken 100 records.

The relative frequency for some of the numbers is shown in the table.

Number	0	1	2	3
Relative frequency	0.4	0.12	0.25	

Ask:

a What is the missing relative frequency?

b How many times did Sam pick each number out of the bag?

c In fact there are actually 80 counters with a 0 inside the bag. Use the table to estimate the number of counters with a 2.

d Why is this answer only an estimate?

Answers:

a 0.23

b 40, 12, 25 and 23

c 50

d This is based on experimental probability values.

Learn 9.3

3 Peter throws a fair 8-sided dice numbered 1–8 and Quinlan flips a fair coin.

Ask students to show all the possible outcomes for the combined events in a list or table. They should explain why the outcomes are mutually exclusive (revises earlier work).

a They should use their list or table to write down the probability that:

  i Peter throws a 7

  ii Quinlan's coin lands on tails

  iii Peter throws a 7 AND Quinlan's coin lands on tails.

b How do the results for **i**, **ii** and **iii** prove that the two events are independent?

Answers:

a i $\frac{1}{8}$ **ii** $\frac{1}{2}$ **iii** $\frac{1}{16}$

b $\frac{1}{8} \times \frac{1}{2} = \frac{1}{16}$ *thus multiplying the individual probabilities gives the overall probability which shows the events involved must be independent.*

Learn 9.4

4 Can students tell you if the following is true of false?

From a pack of cards, Jo has taken four hearts, five diamonds and six clubs. She puts them all face down on a table, then she picks one at random and puts it on one side. She then picks another one at random.

a P(first card is not a ♥) = $\frac{11}{15}$

b P(first card is a ♥, second is a ♦) = $\frac{4}{15} \times \frac{5}{15}$

c P(both ♣) = $\frac{6}{15} \times \frac{6}{15}$

Explain why two of these are false and then give the correct answers.

Answers:

b *After one heart removed, there are still five diamonds but only 14 cards, so P(♥, ♦) = $\frac{4}{15} \times \frac{5}{14}$*

c *After one club removed, there are only five clubs and only 14 cards, so P(♣, ♣) = $\frac{6}{15} \times \frac{5}{14}$ The second probability is dependent on the first outcome.*

Learn... 9.1 Mutually exclusive events

Mutually exclusive events are events that cannot happen at the same time.

The sum of all the probabilities of mutually exclusive events = 1

For example, the following events are mutually exclusive:

- getting a head and getting a tail when a coin is flipped once
- getting a three and getting an even number when a dice is rolled once
- sleeping and running the marathon at the same time
- flying a plane and swimming the Channel at the same time.

For mutually exclusive events, A and B:

P(A or B) = P(A) + P(B). This is known as the OR rule.

P(A) is just a quick way of saying the probability of A, and so on.

So, for example, P(Head or Tail) = P(head) + P(tail)

Other events are not mutually exclusive and can happen at the same time.

For example, the following events are not mutually exclusive:

- getting a four and getting an even number when a dice is rolled
- getting a red card and getting an ace when a card is taken from a pack (e.g. you could get the ace of hearts)
- driving a car and listening to the radio
- eating a meal and watching TV.

Example: Eight cards are face down on a table.

Each card has a picture on its face.

The pictures are:

a red apple, a green apple, a yellow banana, a green frog, a green lizard, a brown frog, a blue dress and a red car.

One card is turned over at **random**, what is the probability that it is a card with:

a a green item on it

b an item that is not green on it

c a frog on it

d an item that is not a frog on it

e a green item or a frog. Give your answer in its simplest form.

Solution: **a** Probability of an event happening = $\dfrac{\text{number of outcomes for that event}}{\text{total number of possible outcomes}}$

Probability of a green item $= \dfrac{3}{8}$ — there are three cards with green items on — there are eight cards altogether

b Probability of an event happening = $\dfrac{\text{number of outcomes for that event}}{\text{total number of possible outcomes}}$

Probability of not a green item $= \dfrac{5}{8}$ — there are five cards without green items on — there are eight cards altogether

Alternatively, if mutually exclusive events cover all the possibilities, their probabilities total 1.

Here, every card has to either have a green item on or **not** a green item on.

The probability of picking a green item + the probability of not picking a green item = 1

So, the probability of not picking a green item = 1 – the probability of picking a green item.

Probability of not picking a green item $= 1 - \dfrac{3}{8} = \dfrac{5}{8}$

c Probability of an event happening = $\dfrac{\text{number of outcomes for that event}}{\text{total number of possible outcomes}}$

Probability of a frog $= \dfrac{2}{8}$ — there are two cards with a frog on

d $1 - \dfrac{2}{8} = \dfrac{6}{8}$ (probability of not picking a frog is 1 – probability of picking a frog)

e The probability of a card with a green item or a frog on is **not** $\dfrac{3}{8} + \dfrac{2}{8}$

This would count the green frog card twice!

This confirms that only the probabilities of mutually exclusive events can be added.

Here you should use the list – there are four cards with either a green item or a frog on them (green apple, green frog, green lizard and brown frog) out of the eight possible outcomes.

So, the probability is $\frac{4}{8}$

Remember that the question for this part asked for the fraction in its simplest form.

Probability $= \frac{1}{2}$

Teacher notes

It is important to realise that word descriptions of probabilities (as opposed to the words 'unlikely', etc.) are not accepted in the examination. For example, 3 out of 4, 3 in 4 or 3:4 would not score any marks under any circumstances for probabilities. Early checking that none of the students are attempting to use these forms is essential. Regarding the notation of P( ), it is important to note that this notation is **not** a requirement for the examination but it is an acceptable shorthand for the probability of an event.

This section is about mutually exclusive events but that term will not be used in the examination. However, it is very helpful for students to understand the term and could well help them to remember the difficult concept of when probabilities can be added and when they cannot.

In any given probability situation, the total probability is always 1.

More accurately, students should know that the sum of all mutually exclusive probabilities in any situation = 1.

Common errors

✗ Adding probabilities when events are not mutually exclusive.

✗ Errors made when adding fractions – remind students that a calculator is available in this unit and thus no addition of fractions really needs to be done using written methods unless trivial. Remind them to check their work on a calculator if they have not used one initially.

AQA Examiner's tip

If the question in the exam does not ask students to provide an answer in its simplest form, then there is no need to cancel. Incorrect cancelling after a correct answer is seen will only be penalised if the simplest form is asked for, but if students cancel incorrectly without the original answer shown they will lose marks.

In the examination the words 'mutually exclusive' will not be used.

However, students need to understand how events happening at the same time affect probabilities.

Learn... 9.2 Relative frequency

The probabilities so far have all been theoretical probabilities.

Theoretical probability is the probability of an event based on expectation (or theory).

Experimental probability is the probability of an event based on testing (or experiment). A probability experiment is a test in which a number of **trials** are performed. The experimental probability is also called the **relative frequency**.

$$\text{Relative frequency of an event} = \frac{\text{number of times an event has happened}}{\text{total number of trials}}$$

Example: Anna picks a counter out of a bag and puts it back after noting the colour.

She does this 100 times.

The graph shows the relative frequency of a black counter after every 10 picks up to the 90th pick.

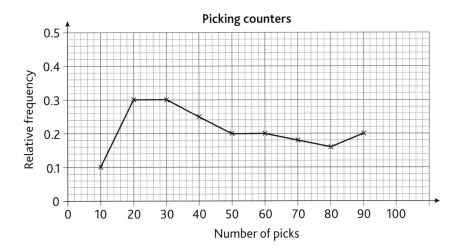

a How many black counters did she get in the first 10 picks?

b How many black counters did she get in the first 90 picks?

c In the final 10 picks she obtained 4 black counters.

How should the graph be completed?

d Obtain the best possible estimate of the probability of a black counter from the information in this question.

Solution:

a 1 (relative frequency of 0.1 is the same as $\frac{1}{10}$ meaning 1 out of the first 10 picks was a black counter)

b 18 (relative frequency of 0.2 after 90 picks indicates $90 \times 0.2 = 18$ black counters)

c The additional 4 black counters picked in the final 10 picks gives a total of 22 out of the 100 picks altogether. Therefore, the final plot should be at a relative frequency of 0.22

The complete graph is therefore as shown below.

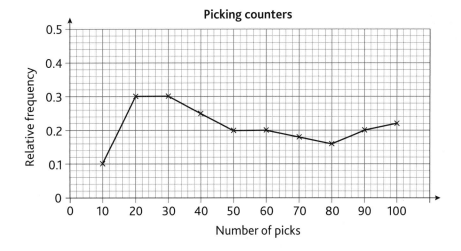

d The best (most reliable) estimate is the one obtained with the greatest amount of data. This is after 100 picks. The relative frequency after 100 picks is 0.22 so the probability of obtaining a black counter is best estimated as 0.22

Teacher notes

This is a very badly done topic in the examination. Very few students seem to see the word 'relative' in relative frequency and when asked to give the relative frequency of an event, simply offer the frequency as the answer.

Furthermore, the differences between theoretical probabilities (the expected chance of an event if all the events are equally likely) and experimental probabilities (using the relative frequency of an event to predict its chances of happening on a further occasion) do not seem to be well understood.

Other important issues here are that the more an experiment is carried out, the more reliable the information gained from it is likely to be. This is a better understood concept and seems logical in that it mirrors work on sample sizes from Chapter 3. The bigger the sample, the more strength can be assigned to any evidence about the population. Finally, the knowledge that repeated experiments do not always give the same results is an important concept. Students may understand this as some real life parallels are formed, e.g. every time you throw two coins you do not get the same result. The starter for 9.2 will also support understanding in these areas.

Common errors

✗ Expecting experiments to give exactly the same results every time and thinking that the results will be the same as the theoretical probability.

✗ Writing frequencies when relative frequencies have been asked for.

AQA Examiner's tip

Remind students that relative frequencies should be given as fractions or decimals, not whole numbers.

Bump up your grade

To get a Grade C, students need to understand relative frequencies and work with them successfully.

 Learn... 9.3 **Independent events and tree diagrams**

Events are **independent** if the outcome of one event does not affect the outcome of the other.

If two events are independent, then the probability that they will both happen is found by multiplying their probabilities together.

This can be written as P(A and B) = P(A) × P(B). This is known as the AND rule.

So, a dice showing an even number and a coin showing a head are independent events. Getting a six on successive throws of a fair dice are also independent events.

A **tree diagram** is a useful tool for showing probabilities.

The probabilities are written on the branches of the tree.

Example: Two fair coins are thrown at the same time.

Find the probability that both coins show a tail.

Solution: The event getting a tail on one coin and getting a tail on the other coin are independent as the outcome of one coin has no influence on the outcome of the other.

The probability of a tail on both coins

= the probability of a tail on the first AND a tail on the second

$$= \frac{1}{2} \times \frac{1}{2}$$

$$= \frac{1}{4}$$

Example: The probability that Wayne scores one goal in a match he plays is 0.4

He plays in the next two matches.

a Draw a tree diagram to show all the possible outcomes and their probabilities.

b Use the tree diagram to find the probability that he scores in neither of his next two games.

Solution: **a** S = scores N = does not score

Match 1	Match 2	Outcome	Probability

S

0.4 ⟍ S ⟋ 0.4 ⟶ S   SS   0.4 × 0.4 = 0.16

0.6 ⟶ N   SN   0.4 × 0.6 = 0.24

0.6 ⟍ N ⟋ 0.4 ⟶ S   NS   0.6 × 0.4 = 0.24

0.6 ⟶ N   NN   0.6 × 0.6 = 0.36

b To not score on both matches means not scoring on Match 1 **AND** not scoring on Match 2.

The events are independent so these probabilities can be multiplied.

Probability of not scoring in both matches = 0.6 × 0.6 = 0.36

Teacher notes

Two important ideas come into this Learn. The notion of independence between events and the use of tree diagrams as an aid to calculating probabilities.

Independence is not a well-understood concept and some simple examples should help understanding. Two events from the same trial cannot be independent – can the students explain why?

AND can be associated with multiplying the probabilities of events that are independent.

For example, in part **b** above, not scoring in both matches means not scoring in the first match AND not scoring in the second match, the probabilities were multiplied.

OR can be associated with adding the probabilities of mutually exclusive events.

For example, on a dice, looking at the the probability of a 3 OR a 5, the probabilities are added.

Common errors

✗ Probabilities not adding to one on every pair of branches.

✗ Probabilities not adding to one for the full set of possible outcomes.

✗ Not getting the structure of the tree diagram correct.

✗ Not writing the probabilities on the branches, instead writing them at the end.

Bump up your grade

To get a Grade C, students need to know when to use the 'AND' rule and when to use the 'OR' rule.

AQA Examiner's tip

Students struggle when examination questions require them to construct their own tree diagrams. It would help if students practise getting the structure of tree diagrams correct before they turn their attention to getting the correct probabilities on the branches.

Learn... 9.4 Dependent events and conditional probability

Events are **dependent** if the outcome of one event affects the outcome of the other. This is also known as **conditional probability**.

Many examples of conditional probability involve choosing items and not replacing them, for example, counters from bags, students from classes, etc.

Again, a tree diagram is a useful tool for showing probabilities.

As before, the probabilities are written on the branches of the tree.

Example: A restaurant has 15 desserts remaining one evening. Of these, 10 are hot desserts, the rest are cold.

The next two customers choose a dessert at random.

a Work out the probability that both desserts chosen are cold. Give your answer in its simplest form.

b Use a tree diagram to show all the possible outcomes and their probabilities.

Solution: **a** The probability that both desserts are cold

= probability 1st dessert is cold AND 2nd dessert is cold

= probability 1st dessert is cold × probability 2nd dessert is cold

$$= \frac{5}{15} \times \frac{4}{14} \longleftarrow$$ only four cold desserts left as the first one is not replaced

only 14 desserts left altogether as the first one is not replaced

$$= \frac{20}{210} = \frac{2}{21}$$

b

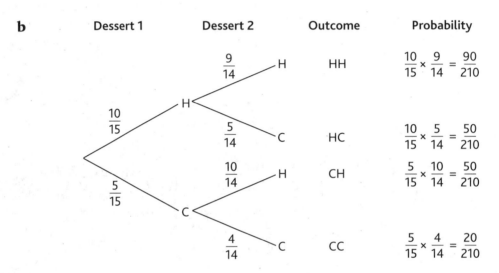

	Dessert 1	Dessert 2	Outcome	Probability

$$\frac{9}{14} \quad H \qquad HH \qquad \frac{10}{15} \times \frac{9}{14} = \frac{90}{210}$$

$$\frac{10}{15}$$

$$\frac{5}{14} \quad C \qquad HC \qquad \frac{10}{15} \times \frac{5}{14} = \frac{50}{210}$$

$$\frac{10}{14} \quad H \qquad CH \qquad \frac{5}{15} \times \frac{10}{14} = \frac{50}{210}$$

$$\frac{5}{15}$$

$$\frac{4}{14} \quad C \qquad CC \qquad \frac{5}{15} \times \frac{4}{14} = \frac{20}{210}$$

Teacher notes

Though this is A* work, there is an intuitive aspect to conditional probability and quite a few students do have some feeling for this, where they appreciate the reduction in the values on the fraction such as $\frac{10}{15}$ becoming $\frac{9}{14}$ above. That said, it needs clear and careful explanation about the reducing values on the numerators and denominators to reinforce the ideas. Usually, conditional probability questions at this level are best approached using a tree diagram, which allows and encourages students to think carefully about the changing probabilities by placing them on the appropriate branches of the tree diagram. The examination uses the term 'without replacement' to indicate that the first item is not put back before the second item is chosen where applicable, but in the example above students had to appreciate that once one dessert was chosen the numbers had reduced.

 Common errors

✗ Not appreciating when the context turns a 'replacement' situation into a 'without replacement' situation.

✗ Cancelling answers incorrectly without showing the unsimplified fraction first.

AQA Examiner's tip

In all tree diagrams, students should remember and check that:

The probabilities on any given pair of branches must add up to 1.

The total probability of all the final outcomes should also be 1.

Fractions and decimals

Practise... **1.1 One quantity as a fraction of another**

1 a $\frac{1}{2}$ **c** $\frac{1}{3}$ **e** $\frac{1}{13}$
  b $\frac{1}{20}$ **d** $\frac{1}{6}$ **f** $\frac{2}{13}$

2 No; Kevin has worked out 50 as a fraction of 500, which is $\frac{1}{10}$

  50p as a fraction of £500 is 50 as a fraction of 50 000, which is $\frac{1}{1000}$

3 a i $\frac{1}{2}$ **ii** $\frac{1}{2}$ **iii** $\frac{1}{2}$
  b $\frac{1}{4}$

4 a i $\frac{1}{2}$ **iii** $\frac{13}{28}$ **v** $\frac{5}{7}$
    ii $\frac{3}{7}$ **iv** $\frac{9}{14}$
  b 21

c The number of students passing can never be more than the number taking the test.

5 a $\frac{3}{8}$ **b** $\frac{5}{8}$

6 a $\frac{1}{6}$ **c** $\frac{7}{10}$ **e** 80
  b $\frac{3}{10}$ **d** 54

7 a $\frac{1}{10}$ **b** $\frac{1}{5}$ **c** $\frac{1}{x}$

8 a $\frac{2}{3}$ **b** UK   **c** ~~Greece~~ SPAIN

  d No; the fractions would not be changed if the vertical axis was scaled differently.

9 48, 49, 50, 51, 52, 53 or 54

Practise... **1.2 Calculating with fractions**

1 $\frac{59}{60}$

2 60

3 ~~45~~

4 a $\frac{15}{16}, \frac{31}{32}$ **c** The sum will become closer to 1.
  b $\frac{1023}{1024}$

5 Tees R Us: £5; Getting Shirty: £5.40

6 a £18   **c** £18.74
  b £52.49   **d** 67p

7 a $4\frac{1}{4}$ yards   **b** $63.75

8 $1\frac{2}{7}$ seconds

9 No, not quite; total needed is $3\frac{1}{24}$ cups.

10 $14\frac{3}{8}$ yards

11 a i A is bigger as A divided by 5 is the same as B divided by 4.
    ii 5, 4; 10, 8; 15, 12; 20, 16; 25, 20, etc. (plus non-integer answers) There is an infinite number of pairs.
    iii The answer is always $\frac{5}{4}$
  b ~~$\frac{8}{9}$~~ $\frac{9}{8}$

12 55 cm

Practise... **1.3 Rounding**

1 a i 2000   **iii** 30   **v** 200
    ii 500   **iv** 6   **vi** 0.01
  b i 1700   **iii** 26   **v** 150
    ii 530   **iv** 5.6   **vi** 0.014

2 a 734 522 to three s.f. is 735 000
  b 1442 to the nearest 10 is 1440
  c 25.60 to the nearest whole number is 26

3 35, 53; 36, 54

4 £52.87

5 a £1.03
  b £23.90 would have been rounded to the nearest penny.

6 a i 57 kg   **ii** 56.5 kg   **iii** 56.7 kg
  b i 26.23   **ii** 3 kg

Practise... **1.4 Upper and lower bounds**

1 a 15.5, 14.5   **d** 4.5, 3.5
  b 157.5, 156.5   **e** 0.5, −0.5
  c 100.5, 99.5

2 a 100.5 cm³, 99.5 cm³   **d** 1000.5 cm³, 999.5 cm³
  b 15.5 cm³, 14.5 cm³   **e** 500.5 cm³, 499.4 cm³
  c 245.5 cm³, 244.5 cm³

3 257.5 km

4 65.75 kg

5 a i 10.75 cm, 10.25 cm
 ii 7.25 cm, 6.75 cm

 iii 23.75 cm, 23.25 cm
 iv 15.25 cm, 14.75 cm

6 37.75 g, 37.25 g.

7 Yes. Measured to the nearest gram.

Practise... 1.5 Calculating with bounds

1 36 cm

2 No; the upper bound of the length is 93.5 cm so the length could be, for example, 93.495 cm.

3 7.661 m/s

4 2.94 hours

5 a 13   **b** 11

6 Upper bound of total weight is 191.25 kg so it is not safe to use the hoist.

7 Maximum difference is 20 g, minimum difference is 18 g.

8 a and d as big as possible and b and c as small as possible.

9 Yes, 5% of 5.3 mm is less than 0.5 mm.

10 No, the tube could have a diameter as small as 4.86 mm.

11 118.47 pounds

Assess 1

1 $\frac{1}{5}$

2 £1050

3 a $\frac{7}{12}$ **b** $\frac{1}{3}$

4 a $\frac{1}{2}$ **b** $\frac{4}{7}$

5 a 8   **c** 21

 b $6\frac{13}{18}$ **d** £21.20

6 a e.g. **i** 124, 137.2   **ii** 0.012, 0.014792
 b e.g. **i** 121.9, 123   **ii** 0.123, 0.12185

7 £49.49, £48.50

8 12 years, 364 days (or 365 if it is a leap year), 23 hours, 59 minutes, 59 seconds, ...

9 $14.75 \leqslant l < 15.25$

10 50.92 litres, but it could be as much as 51.23 litres or as little as 50.65 litres

11 8 cm

12 Just. The least weight of the sweets is 97.5 g.

13 a 277 kg
 b No; the weight could be as much as 352 kg.

14 10 950

15 6.71 m/s

AQA Examination-style questions

1 16 mm

2 Indices and standard index form

Practise... 2.1 Rules of indices

1 a 100   **d** 200
 b 1 000 000   **e** 990
 c 1   **f** 10

2 a 10^4 **d** 10^1
 b 10^7 **e** 10^{-1}
 c 10^2 **f** 10^{-3}

3 a False. $10^2 = 100$

b False. $10^{-1} = \frac{1}{10}$

c True. $10^{50} \times 10^{50} = 10^{50+50} = 10^{100}$

d False. $1\,000\,000^0 = 1$

4 a 10^4
b 10^8

5 a 10^{11} **d** 10^6
b 10^{11} **e** $\frac{1}{10^3}$
c 10^4 **f** 10^{10}

g 10^6 **l** $\frac{1}{10^3}$
h 10^6 **m** 10^2
i $\frac{1}{10^6}$ **n** 10^2
j $\frac{1}{10^6}$ **o** 10^0
k 10^8

Practise... 2.2 Standard form

1 a 3.7×10^3 **e** 3.5×10 **i** 2×10^{-11}
b 2.3×10^7 **f** 5×10^{-3} **j** 5×10^{-1}
c 2.002×10^5 **g** 1.3×10^{-1}
d 8.5×10^9 **h** 1.78×10^{-7}

2 a 7000 **e** 76.635 **i** 0.0003086
b 7000 **f** 510 000 000 **j** 0.0000000066
c 42 000 **g** 0.3
d 608.5 **h** 0.00125

3 3.84×10^8

4 a 9×10^{12} **f** 2.5×10^{-7} **k** 3.5×10^6
b 1.6×10^{15} **g** 2×10^8 **l** 8.08×10^4
c 8.4×10^{12} **h** 3×10^{13} **m** 4.68×10^4
d 2.821×10^{13} **i** 5×10^{-10}
e 2.25×10^{14} **j** 4×10^{-9}

5 4.8×10^{-5}, 0.00048, 4.8×10^{-3}, 4800, 4.8×10^4, 480000

6 perimeter $= 3.24 \times 10^4$ m
area $= 3.08 \times 10^7$ m^2

7 4.4×10^{23} m

8 1.81×10^{14} m (3 s.f.)

9 a 1 000 000 000 **c** 1.99×10^9
b 1×10^3

10 4.25×10^3

11 9.6×10^{-3} cm

Assess 2

1 a 10^3 **c** 10^1 **e** 10^{-3}
b 10^8 **d** 10^{-1} **f** 10^{-7}

2 a 10^{17} **d** 10^6 **g** 10^{21}
b 10^9 **e** 10^0 **h** 10^{20}
c 10^5 **f** 10^{-5} **i** 10^{-8}

3 a and b Pacific Ocean: 165 000 000 km^2
Atlantic Ocean: 82 400 000 km^2
Arctic Ocean: 14 000 000 km^2
Mediterranean Sea: 2 500 000 km^2
Gulf of Mexico: 1 540 000 km^2

4 a 1.1×10^8 is bigger
b i $n = 5$ **ii** $n = 1$ **iii** $n = 5$

5 1.5625×10^{-2}

6 1.2×10^{10}

7 a i 3×10^{-3} **ii** 6.55×10^{-6} **iii** 1×10^{-1}
b i 0.000000001 **iii** 0.000039958
ii 0.00000422
c 77.44
d 16 000 000

8 a 3.17×10^5 **b** 4.77×10^{12} **c** 4.1×10^{-18}

9 1 081 000 litres or 1.081×10^6 litres

10 3.6

11 0.0825 g

12 a 1.10×10^{12} km^2
b 5.44×10^{12}

AQA Examination-style questions

1 a 36 is not between 1 and 10.
b 6.55 (3 s.f.)

3 Collecting data

Practise... 3.1 Types of data

1

Person	Qualitative	Quantitative	Discrete	Continuous	Primary	Secondary
Nat		✓	✓			✓
Prita		✓	✓		✓	
Niles	✓				✓	

2 **a** discrete **d** discrete **g** continuous
    b discrete **e** continuous **h** continuous
    c continuous **f** discrete **i** discrete

3 **a** A sample is a part of the population that it is hoped has the same features as the population.

    b to save time and money

    c Items may be 'used up' when sampled so this does not want to be too large scale or items are wasted. Also, it is time consuming and possibly expensive to take a particularly large sample.

4 (many possible answers)

    a the colour/style/type of pattern

    b number of goals scored/league position/match attendance

    c speed/time to leave Earth's atmosphere/age of astronauts

    d your mark/your answers/your feelings when doing it

    e life expectancy/types of rat food/average length it might grow to

5 Answers depend upon the information obtained from newspaper or internet.

6 How: a sample from the production line needs to be taken across several time periods – it is not sufficient to simply test, say, the first 20 bulbs produced one morning. May make mention of use of random sampling in answer.

Why: Testing will use up the light bulbs so testing the whole population would mean there were no light bulbs left (which would leave everyone in the dark).

Practise... 3.2 Data collection methods

1 When rewriting the questions, there are many possible options.

    a Too few groups and no box for an answer of 1 hour.

      Rewrite response boxes with groups.

      Less than 1 hour/1 or more but less than 2/2 or more but less than 3/3 or more.

    b only two of many choices

      It is probably best to rewrite this as an open question asking for their own answer as there are so many possible options.

    c Most people will do more than one thing so the question should probably ask which they do most.

      Which of these do you do most of in your leisure time? (tick one box)

      Then offer same choices plus the choice of 'other'.

    d A biased question leading people into saying 'yes'. Options could also be better.

      Do you like football? Yes I love it/Yes I quite like it/No, I am not keen/No, I hate it!

    e This is a personal question that should be avoided unless essential. If it had to be asked, additional options should be offered.

      less than £10 000/£10 000 to £19 999/£20 000 to £29 999/£30 000 to £39 999/£40 000 or more

    f The question needs a time scale so that everyone is not left to judge how often 'rarely' and 'sometimes' is. Also, anyone who never goes cannot answer.

      How often do you go to the cinema in a typical month?

      Never/Once/Twice/Three times/More than three times

g Too black and white, it would be more useful to find out how much/often.

How often do you travel by taxi?

Every day/More than once a week/More than once a month/Less than once a month/Never. (In some ways, some of these options overlap but this is a frequently used type of scale.)

h Opinion of question writer is in the question.

What do you think of dogs?

Love them/Like them a little/Do not particularly like them/Totally dislike them/Don't know

2 a data logging (3i below)

b online questionnaire (email questionnaire) (3ii below)

c controlled experiment (3iii below)

d face-to-face (or personal) interview (3iv below)

e observation (3v below)

3 a i Does not need a person to be employed to carry out this check.

ii He can do it at his own convenience.

iii He is collecting the data himself so will be content it is accurate.

iv Data is obtained straight away.

v should be accurate and complete

b i may break down

ii He may decide not to do it/make up answers.

iii time consuming work

iv Annie may not like interviews or be in a rush.

v Students may not behave normally if being watched and recorded.

4 to check that the questions in a questionnaire give the type of response desired

to check that questions are understood

to check the way that data is collected works

5 a i Are you married? Yes ☐ No ☐

ii Which is your favourite holiday destination?

UK ☐ France ☐ Spain ☐ USA ☐ Greece ☐ Other ☐

iii How many hours sleep did you get last night?

3 or less ☐ 4–5 ☐ 6–7 ☐ 8–9 ☐ 10 or more ☐

iv What pets do you own?

Cat ☐ Dog ☐ Rabbit ☐ Bird ☐ Other ☐ None ☐

b i Are you married? _____

ii Which is your favourite holiday destination? _____

iii How many hours sleep did you get last night? _____

iv What pets do you own? _____

c Closed questions are better for collecting data that can be analysed easily. Open questions lead to many different answers being given.

6 Note: This is not easy – focus carefully on exactly what was to be found out.

a In the last two years, have you been on a holiday?

Yes ☐   No ☐   Don't Know ☐

If Yes, tick which of these places you have been to.

UK ☐   France ☐   Spain ☐ USA ☐   Greece ☐ Other ☐ (please state where) _____

b

What is your gender?

Male ☐   Female ☐

How old are you?

Under 10 ☐   10–14 ☐   15–19 ☐ 20–29 ☐   30–39 ☐   40+ ☐

Do you like Wayne Rooney?

Yes ☐   No ☐ Don't know ☐

c Does someone in your family buy a newspaper?

Yes ☐   No ☐   Don't know ☐

If yes, how much does it cost?

Under 30p ☐   30p–39p ☐ 40p–49p ☐   50p or more ☐ Don't know ☐

Practise... 3.3 Organising data

1 a 25   **c** 15
b 41   **d** observation

2

	Sheep	Cattle	Pigs
Male	80	170	90
Female	50	70	140

3 a i

	Apple	Strawberry	Banana	Orange	Other
Y10 girl					
Y10 boy					

ii

	Black	Brown	Blonde	Red	Other
Male					
Female					

iii

	Full (100%)	Quite full (75%)	Half full (50%)	Nearly empty (25%)	Empty
Morning					
Evening					

b i A student may not have a single favourite or may not like fruit at all.

ii Many people do not have hair of one colour or what one person may call brown, another may judge to be red. Also in observation situations, it is often reported that it can be difficult to judge whether a person is male or female at times.

iii judging the 'fullness' of a bus as it passes you and categorising the fullness in the first place

4

Weather	Morning	Afternoon
Sunshine		
Cloudy (dry)		
Raining		
Snow / sleet / hail		
Other		

5 a 7 April to 5 June would cost £124 + £124 + £89 + £0 = £337, which is OK.

6 June to 21 July would cost £168 + £168 + £120 + £12 = £468, which is OK.

22 July to 5 Sept would cost £215 + £215 + £199 + £50 = £679, which is too much.

So they could go on their holiday any time between 7 April and 21 July.

b Yes, he is right. If they had £700, this would cover 2 × £337 = £674 and they could have 2 weeks between 7 April and 5 June.

Practise... 3.4 Sampling methods

1 Sample depends on the random numbers used.

2 a Year 10 = 15   Year 11 = 15
Year 12 = 11   Year 13 = 9

b Give each student a number and then, using a calculator or tables, obtain random numbers. Match the random numbers to the students in the list.

3 a Management = 2, Sales = 26, Security = 5, Office = 7

b Give the office staff numbers from 01 to 35. Use calculators or the random numbers table to obtain seven different values between 01 and 35. Match these values to the office staff.

4 Social Science = 8 (rounded from 8.205 ...)

The Arts = 3 (rounded from 2.852 ...)

Science = 6 (rounded from 6.382 ...)

Sport and Leisure = 3 (rounded from 2.561 ...)

5 a to get a fair proportion from each age group, as children in different age groups will probably have different views

b by gender or perhaps by household income

c age 5–7 = 18 (rounded from 18.075 ...)

age 8–10 = 25 (rounded from 24.648 ...)

age 11–13 = 31 (rounded from 31.221 ...)

age 14–16 = 26 (rounded from 26.056 ...)

6 Answers will vary according to the random numbers used.

7 Year 7 = 23.394 before rounding

Year 8 = 21.189 before rounding

Year 9 = 19.271 before rounding

Year 10 = 18.696 before rounding

Year 11 = 17.450 before rounding

If these are all rounded to nearest integer, the total would be 99. Round the Year 11 value up, not down as this was nearest to rounding up initially out of those rounded down.

Final sample Year 7 = 23, Year 8 = 21, Year 9 = 19, Year 10 = 19, Year 11 = 18

8 Use a stratified random sample.

800 components should be from Machine A, 700 from Machine B and 500 from Machine C.

For each machine, try to get the output numbered in some way so that a random selection can be obtained using random numbers. Alternatively, perhaps a sample could be taken at particular time intervals.

9 Number of members

	Adults	Children
Male	1323	567
Female	3003	1001

Number in sample of 200

	Adults	Children
Male	45 (44.893)	19 (19.240)
Female	102 (101.900)	34 (33.967)

Assess 3

1 a 24   **c** $\frac{19}{40}$

b 27   **d** 50%

2 a

	Chocolate	Sweets
Male	24	26
Female	16	4

b 20   **d** $\frac{16}{40} = \frac{2}{5}$

c 70   **e** 3

3 a continuous   **d** continuous   **g** discrete
b discrete   **e** discrete
c discrete   **f** continuous

4 a i It would be very difficult to remember accurately.

ii need to offer choices regarding how often they are watched

b i This is biased with words *our* and *improved*.

Rate the fruit juice you have just had.

Excellent/Good/Average/Poor/Terrible

ii A personal question. What is your monthly salary? (Again could probably offer choices.)

iii A leading question. Give your opinion on the new bypass (with choices).

iv A leading question. Do you prefer smoking or non-smoking areas?

v No time period is specified. How many showers do you have in a typical week? (Options possible again.)

5 a Take a sample of 20–40 sheep from throughout the farm and weigh them, finding the average.

b Ask random people from the town, using a phone, postal or face-to-face interview.

c Question a sample of students from across the school in different classes.

d Measure the hand spans of a sample of students from your school, including all ages and genders.

e Take a sample of villagers and ask them. Perhaps go from door to door to ensure a variety of the homes within the village.

f Phone, postal or email survey with a carefully chosen and unbiased sample.

g Use a data-logging machine to keep a full record. This should enable an accurate result for this data.

6 Write a hypothesis such as 'this shop is the cheapest in town for fruit and vegetables'.

Collect data by finding a sample of fruit and vegetables from this shop and from other fruit and vegetable sellers in the town.

For each selected item, calculate measures of average and spread, and show prices in simple diagrams such as bar charts and pictograms.

Interpret the data, the measures and the diagrams, and decide whether they support the hypothesis or not.

7 Answer will depend upon random numbers chosen.

8 a A random sample would not be appropriate as it is not likely to give sufficient weighting to management, office and sales staff.

b The sample needs to be chosen so that the proportions represent those of the population as a whole.

Occupation	Management	Office	Sales	Shop Floor
Number	10	15	30	145
Fraction	$\frac{10}{200}$	$\frac{15}{200}$	$\frac{30}{200}$	$\frac{145}{200}$
For a sample size of 20	$\frac{10}{200} \times 20 =$ 1 worker	$\frac{15}{200} \times 20 =$ 1.5 workers	$\frac{30}{200} \times 20 =$ 3 workers	$\frac{145}{200} \times 20 =$ 14.5 workers
For a sample size of 35	$\frac{10}{200} \times 35 =$ 1.75 workers	$\frac{15}{200} \times 35 =$ 2.625 workers	$\frac{30}{200} \times 35 =$ 5.25 workers	$\frac{145}{200} \times 35 =$ 25.375 workers

In the case of the sample of 20, it is important to round 1.5 and 14.5 for sampling purposes. If both numbers are rounded up, the sample size is 21. You are told the sample size is 20 so you need to round one up and one down to get the right total; it doesn't matter which.

AQA Examination-style questions

Age (years)	10–24	25–44	45–60	61+
Number of members	150	198	132	120
Number in sample	25	33	22	20

4 Percentages

Practise... 4.1 Percentages, fractions and decimals

1 a $\frac{16}{25}$ **b** 6.6875

2 $\frac{19}{40}$

3 No. $\frac{1}{3} = 33.3\%$ (or $33\frac{1}{3}\%$) and 34% is more than this.

4 a

To find	20%	1%	12%	35%	
Multiply	0.2	0.01	0.12	0.35	
To find	7%	4%	17.5%	2.5%	125%
Multiply	0.07	0.04	0.175	0.025	1.25

b **i** 30 **iv** £175 **vii** £26.25
   ii 1.6 **v** £1.40 **viii** £0.81
   iii 38.4 **vi** £8.80 **ix** £32

5 £1210

6 0.874 million or 874 000

7 **a** £80.50 **b** £10.26 **c** £13.30

8 **a** £10.88 **b** £5.69

9 No – the multiplier should be 0.06 not 0.6

10 **a** 70% **b** 6p **c** £1.80

11 $\frac{2}{3}$ of £1 million

12 **a** 390 **b** $\frac{1}{5}$

13 **a** £1950 **b** £5899

14 £16.25

15

	Working age	Retirement age
Men	200	43
Women	183	74

16 Carrie (Amie gets £20, Ben gets £36, Carrie gets £43.20, Dave gets £40.32 and Emma & Fergus get £30.24 each.)

17 **a** 150 **b** 57

Practise... 4.2 Increasing or decreasing by a percentage

1 **a**

To increase by	20%	40%	8%	3.5%	12.5%	125%
Multiply by	1.2	1.4	1.08	1.035	1.125	2.25

To decrease by	20%	40%	8%	3.5%	12.5%	1.25%
Multiply by	0.8	0.6	0.92	0.965	0.875	0.9875

b **i** £18 **v** £103.95 **ix** £294.40
   ii £22.40 **vi** £21.60 **x** £241.25
   iii £345.60 **vii** £12 **xi** £80.85
   iv £258.75 **viii** £9.60 **xii** £9.48

2 **a** 126 m **d** 51.25 litres **g** 488.75
   b 91 kg **e** 108 560 **h** £36.50
   c 6.8 miles **f** 24.19

3 **a** £81.64 **b** £10.39 **c** £45

4

Type of house	New price
Terraced	£91 700
Semi	£140 600
Detached	£212 700

5 **a** £468.83 **b** £258.70 **c** £70.49

6

Item	Sale price
Trousers	£32.60
Shirt	£19.67
Jumper	£23.97
Gloves	£11.99

7 **a** The multiplier should be 1.02, not 1.2
   b £17.85

8 No. Final price = £10 × 1.15 × 0.95 = £9.98

9 No.
   1.2 × 1.2 = 1.44, so the increase is 44%

10 £9733.60

11

Job	Number of employees	Salary (per year)	2% increase
Clerical assistant	5	£15 400	£308
Factory worker	25	£16 900	£338
Warehouse worker	8	£17 500	£350
Delivery driver	4	£19 750	£395

The £350 increase will cost the company 42 × £350 = £14 700

The company will prefer the 2% increase, which will cost
5 × £308 + 25 × £338 + 8 × £350 + 4 × £395 = £14 370

Clerical assistants and factory workers will prefer the £350 increase, but delivery drivers will prefer 2%.

Both will give the same to Warehouse workers.

12 The first shop cost will be £441.75

The second shop cost will be £520
The third shop cost will be £439.20

The third shop has the best offer.
Abdul may choose the second shop if he has not got enough money to pay it all at once.

13 **EasyPay Option**

Balance is £395   7.5% of £395 = £29.625

Amount owed = £424.63

Monthly payment = £424.63 ÷ 6 = £70.77

PayLess Option

Month	Balance	Balance + 2.5%	Payment	New Balance
1	395	404.88	50	354.88
2	354.88	363.75*	50	313.75
3	313.75	321.59	50	271.59
4	271.59	278.38	50	228.38
5	228.38	234.09	50	184.09
6	184.09	188.69	50	138.69
7	138.69	142.16	50	92.16
8	92.16	94.46	50	44.46
9	44.46	45.57	45.57	

Total paid in monthly payments = £445.57 in 9 months.

* The amounts in this table have been rounded to the nearest penny. Students may choose to use rounded figures in the calculations or continue calculations on their calculators without rounding. This does not affect the values given above when each is rounded to the nearest penny.

Conclusions: On PayLess, Sally would pay £20.94 more (from £445.57–£424.63) but she would have less to pay each month. It would take her 9 months to pay off her debt, instead of 6 months by EasyPay. If she cannot afford more than £50 per month, then PayLess might be the better option.

If EasyPay charged 8%, it would cost £426.60 and if PayLess charged 1.5% it would cost £423.67.

Practise... 4.3 Successive percentages

1 a 296
 b 222
 c 1480 × 0.2 × 0.75
 d 1110

2 3024

3 £2.70

4 1170

5 £110 124

6 £25 823

7 £10.33 (nearest penny)

8 42.5%

9 a Katie has just added the percentage rises instead of using multipliers.

 b 1.12 × 1.18 = 1.18 × 1.12 = 1.3216
 Both give the same increase but of 32.16% not 30%

10 a 12.5% (to 3 s.f.)   **b** 32.2% (to 3 s.f.)

11 a 61.2%   **b** Saturday
 c cheapest on Saturday, but may not have any left

12 1.3 × 0.75 = 0.975
 The shop makes a loss of 2.5%.

13 20% reduction

Practise... 4.4 Compound interest

1 £661.50

2 £5105.82

3 a i £2676.45   **ii** £3581.70
 b i £676.45   **ii** £905.25
   iii The interest is compounded.

4 £4009.74

5 No. Carmen will have more than 20% more because interest will be paid on the interest. $1.04^5 = 1.2166...$ so Carmen will have nearly 22% more.

6 £32.23 more

7 a

After year	1	2	3	4
Value (nearest £)	£6320	£5056	£4045	£3236
After year	5	6	7	8
Value (nearest £)	2589	£2071	£1657	£1325

b

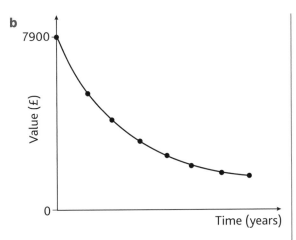

8 a £19 456   **b** £21 392 (nearest £)

   c Wage increases vary according to economic circumstances, she may change jobs, etc.

9 After 4 years £9910.60, after 5 years £10 455.68

10 a 5 years   **b** 12 years

11 a After 10 pay rises, her yearly earnings = £16 000 × 1.02^{10} = £19 504 < £20 000

b After 12 pay rises, her pay will be £20 292 > £20 000

12 After 9 months, Mike's weight = 112 kg × 0.965^9 = 81.3 kg (to 3 s.f.) and after 10 months it is 78.4 kg (to 3 s.f.), so he reaches his target weight after 10 months.

13 Ruby (interest is Emerald £585, Ruby £587.65, Sapphire £584.35)

14

After	10 yrs	20 yrs	30 yrs	40 yrs	50 yrs
Population	20 240	18 621	17 131	15 761	14 500
After	60 yrs	70 yrs	80 yrs	90 yrs	100 yrs
Population	13 340	12 273	11 291	10 388	9557

Assuming constant rate of decrease, population will halve in about 80 years and be less than 10 000 by the end of the century.

15 14%

Practise... 4.5 Writing one quantity as a percentage of another

1 a 65.4% (to 3 s.f.)   **b** 34.6% (to 3 s.f.)

2 12.9% (to 3 s.f.)

3 a 12.5%   **d** 17%   **g** 1.58% (to 3 s.f.)
   b 2.5%   **e** 14%   **h** 7.29% (to 3 s.f.)
   c 5%   **f** 74%

4 a 17.1% (to 3 s.f.)   **b** 82.9% (to 3 s.f.)

5 a 56.3% (to 3 s.f.)   **b** 43.7% (to 3 s.f.)

6 a No, 10 is the frequency, not the percentage.
   b Blonde 33.3%, Brown 43.3%, Black 16.7%, Red 6.7%
   c 33.3% + 43.3% + 16.7% + 6.7% = 100%

7 70.8% (to 3 s.f.)

8 a 71.4% (to 3 s.f.)   **c** 64.3% (to 3 s.f.)
   b 57.1% (to 3 s.f.)   **d** 55.6% (to 3 s.f.)

9 a 46.3%   **b** 12.5%

10 a i 47.1% (to 3 s.f.)   **ii** 52.9% (to 3 s.f.)
   b i 28.8% (to 3 s.f.)   **ii** 39.4% (to 3 s.f.)
   c i 30%   **ii** 49.0% (to 3 s.f.)

11

Cycled	Number of people aged	
	5–15 years	16 years and over
Once or more per week	45%	9%
At least once, but less than once per week	26%	15%
Never	29%	76%

Practise... 4.6 Finding a percentage increase and decrease

1 3.81% (to 3 s.f.)

2 10.5% (to 3 s.f.)

3 a Fall in male workers = 36.9% (to 3 s.f.), less than that in female workers = 54.9% (to 3 s.f.)
   b 41.8% (to 3 s.f.)

4 a i 9.09% (to 3 s.f.)   **ii** 33.7% (to 3 s.f.)
   b 12.5% (to 3 s.f.)

5 a She has divided £30 by £150 instead of by £120.
   b 25%

6 Males increased by 10.9% and females by 12.8% (to 3 s.f.).

7 66.7% (to 3 s.f.).

8 20%

9 a 50% **b** 100% **c** 400%

10 Yes, she is correct with the explanation.

11

Drink	% change
Fruit juice	+ 21.4%
Low calorie soft drinks	+14.9%
Other soft drinks	−15.1%
Beverages (e.g. tea, coffee)	No change
Alcoholic drinks	+1.2%

12 a 2001–2006 (2.5% increase)

b could be answered in a variety of ways

Practise... 4.7 Reverse percentages

1 a £8.95 **c** 260000
b £35

2 a £1250 **b** £375

3 125

4 £2.66

5 Sumira would pay less at Compsave. (PC Perfect charges £585.15 including VAT.)

6 a The 10% saving is based on the full price and £3150 is not the full price (only 90%).

b Kev has saved £350.

7 £5000

8 VAT = £1373.89 (total amount = £9224.69)

9 £9506

Assess 4

1 Test A

Test	Mark
A	65%
B	60%

2 a 20.1% (to 3 s.f.)

b i Some students read more than one of the categories.

ii 86% **iii** 30.4%

3 Girls did better.
Boys 68%, Girls 70%

4 20%

5 £1622.40

6 60% of 135 = 81 marks, so she needs 49 on the second paper.

7 189

8 a 13498 **b** 14 hours (50736)

9 60 mph

10 £295

11 Increase in English:
$75 - 53 = 22$
$22 \div 53 \times 100\% = 41.5\%$
Increase in maths:
$63 - 41 = 22$
$22 \div 41 \times 100\% = 53.7\%$

AQA Examination-style questions

1 $£2000 \times 1.072^{10} = £4008.46$
The money is doubled

5 **Ratio and proportion**

Practise... **5.1** Finding and simplifying ratios

1
a	1:2	**e**	1:6	**i**	3:2	**m**	3:5
b	1:3	**f**	1:7	**j**	1:4	**n**	3:2
c	1:4	**g**	3:1	**k**	1:8	**o**	1:3
d	1:5	**h**	4:3	**l**	3:8	**p**	1:4

2
a	1:2	**d**	8:1	**g**	3:20
b	1:3	**e**	1:20	**h**	16:3
c	2:1	**f**	11:50		

3 e.g. 2:4, 3:6, 10:20
The second number is twice the first.

4
a	2:6	**c**	7:21	**e**	$a:3a$
b	5:15	**d**	1200:3600		

5 1:2.5 0.2:0.5 2:5 3:7.5

6 She is adding the same number to both numbers in the ratio instead of multiplying them both by the same thing.

7 1:10

8 **a** 6 **b** 7

9
a	6	**c**	1.5	**e**	4 and 6
b	8	**d**	$\frac{2}{3}$		

10 many possibilities

11 **a** 2:3
b No, the second photo has ratio 5:7

12
a	1:2, 2:1	**c**	60 g
b	100 g	**d**	$\frac{1}{2}$

13 **a** 1:20, 1:16, 1:17, 1:15, 1:21
b **i** 1000 **ii** 100
c School 4

14 **b** 1:50 000 **c** 1 **d** 3 km

15 Flour 4.5 ounces
Water 7.5 ounces
Eggs 3

16 **a** It increases. Ratio is 1:8, 9:16, 25:24

Practise... **5.2** Dividing quantities in given ratios

1
a	50, 100	**d**	2 litres, 4 litres
b	100, 200	**e**	£0.50, £1
c	£1.50, £3	**f**	0.5 litres, 1 litre

2
a 30, 120; 60, 240; £0.90, £3.60; 1.2 litres, 4.8 litres; £0.30, £1.20; 0.3 litres, 1.2 litres
b 60, 90; 120, 180; £1.80, £2.70; 2.4 litres, 3.6 litres; 60p, 90p
c 45, 105; 90, 210; £1.35, £3.15; 1.8 litres, 4.2 litres; 45p, 105p; 0.45 litres, 1.05 litres
d 15, 30, 105; 30, 60, 210; 60p, £1.20, £3.15; 0.6 litres, 1.2 litres, 4.2 litres; 15p, 30p, £1.05; 0.15 litres, 0.3 litres, 1.05 litres

3 £210

4 162 degrees

5 **a** 50 g, 75 g, 75 g, 40 g, 30 g, 65 g
b chicken sandwich, grilled salmon, yoghurt (whole milk), milk
c 400 g
d taco chips, bread

6 **a** copper 950 g, tin 40 g, zinc 10 g
b copper 9.5 kg, tin 400 g, zinc 100 g
c copper 475 g, tin 20 g, zinc 5 g
d 0.06 g

7 Leena £51 851.85, Kate £18 148.15

8 **a** 375, 375; 400, 500; 800, 1000; 612, 714; 602, 582
b School E; this has the smallest number of girls for one boy.

Practise... **5.3** The unitary method

1 1125 g

2 1.5 hours

3 3 kg

4 £114.75

5 400 g flour, 100 g butter, 125 g cheese

6 15 minutes. A piece of music is the same length no matter how many people are playing it!

7 **a** 317 miles **b** 32 miles **c** 3 hrs 57 minutes

8 **a** 41.3 litres

b 97 miles

c that the rate of consumption of diesel is constant

9 large size

10 **a** £2.85, £2.20, £2.08

b 25.50 kg

c £72.68

d It is cheaper per kilogram. It is heavy to carry, difficult to store, not easy to use, etc.

11 **a** 900 newtons

b 60 newtons

c 1950 newtons

d 6 : 1 : 15

12 **a** £37.50

b

Number of hours worked	0	2	4	6	8	10
Money earned (£)	0	7.50	15	22.50	30	37.50

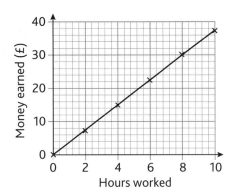

c **i** The amount earned is directly proportional to the hours worked.

ii Read y-coordinate of point where line though (5, 0) parallel to y-axis meets graph.

13 1, 1, 2, 3, 5, 8, 13, 21, 34, 55, 89, 144, 233, 377, 610, 987, 1597, 2584, 4181, 6765, 10946

1 : 1, 1 : 0.5, 1 : 1.5, 1 : 1.67, 1 : 1.6, 1 : 1.625, 1 : 1.619, …

The ratios get gradually get closer to 1 : 1.618

Assess 5

1 1 : 18

2 3 : 7

3 **a** **i** 3 : 4 **iii** 100 : 1 **v** 5 : 7

ii 1 : 3 **iv** 1 : 8

b **i** 2 : 3 **ii** 7 : 10

4 **a** 400 g

b 375 ml

5 **a** the same in each

b 24

6 **a** £4, £8

b £2, £10

c £1.71/£10.29

7 15

8 £1350

9 'Lowerpay'

10 **a** 7 seconds

b 16 seconds

11 **a** Cuba

b Cuba 20 468, Israel 10 140, Italy 107 413, Nigeria 203 558, Tanzania 55 772, Thailand 109 666, UK 109 478, USA 494 999

12 **a** 3.33 l

b Two 2.5 litre cans (£27.96)

AQA Examination-style questions

1 195

6 Statistical measures

Practise... 6.1 Frequency distributions

1 a $\frac{1045}{43} = 24.30$ (2 d.p.)

b 30

c 30

d $40 - 0 = 40$

e $30 - 15 = 15$

f $\frac{20}{43} \times 100 = 46.51$ (2 d.p.)

2 a i 96 **ii** 176

b $\frac{88}{324} = 27.16\%$ (2 d.p.)

c $70 - 20 = 50\,\text{mph}$

d i $60\,\text{mph}$

ii $50\,\text{mph}$

iii $\frac{15\,240}{324} = 47.04\,\text{mph}$ (2 d.p.)

3 a 3.47 **c** 6 **e** $\frac{20}{100} = \frac{1}{5}$

b 3 **d** 5

4 a 1

b 1.5

c The median, as you cannot get 1.5 people in a car.

5 values for other country

mode = 1 median = 1 mean = 1.36

These measures are all smaller than the equivalent value for USA.

Conclude that there are more rumbles of thunder per minute in a storm in USA.

6 many possible answers

7 a

x	f
2	35
4	65
6	19
8	value > 65

b

x	f
2	35
4	65
6	19
8	value 0–80

c

x	f
2	35
4	65
6	19
8	81

d

x	f
2	35
4	65
6	19
8	8

8 Some of the measures that may be calculated are given in the tables below.

Measure	Location	
	Town centre	Village
Mode	2	3
Median	2	3
Mean (2 d.p.)	2.06	3.09
IQR	0	2

Percentage of bedrooms of each size:

Number of bedrooms	% in town sample	% in village sample
1	22.9	8.6
2	54.3	25.7
3	17.1	28.6
4	5.7	22.9
5	0	14.3

Averages suggest fewer bedrooms in a town house than in a village house on average.

Percentages show a much greater percentage for the houses with a small number of bedrooms in a town compared to a village. Many similar comments are possible.

9 a Big Bus: mode = 0, median = 5, mean = 5.75 minutes, IQR = 10, range = 35

Super Express: mode = 5, median = 12.5, mean = 10.7 minutes, IQR = 10, range = 20

Super Express is, on average, more minutes late than Big Bus but Big Bus has a larger range of late times indicating that it can be much later than Super Express when it is late.

b A bus that is on average a little late is unlikely to cause a problem. However, if a bus was extremely late (as indicated as a possibility by a larger range) that would be a problem.

10 The mean of x is 5. So the total (fx) must be 500.

The median of x is 4. So the 50th and 51st values must be 4.

The mode of x is 3. So 3 must have the highest frequency.

The range of x is 7. So the highest take away the lowest must be 7.

One of many possible distributions for x is therefore:

x	Frequency
0	0
1	0
2	0
3	40
4	20
5	2
6	0
7	24
8	14
9	0
10	1

Practise... 6.2 Grouped frequency distributions

1 a $2 \leqslant t < 4$

  b $2 \leqslant t < 4$

  c $\frac{2}{34} \times 100\% = 5.88235\%$

    $= 6\%$ (1 s.f.)

  d

Time, t (minutes)	Frequency	Midpoint, x	fx
$0 \leqslant t < 2$	8	1	8
$2 \leqslant t < 4$	14	3	42
$4 \leqslant t < 6$	6	5	30
$6 \leqslant t < 8$	4	7	28
$8 \leqslant t < 10$	2	9	18

    $126 \div 34 = 3.71$ minutes (2 d.p.)

  e About 10 minutes

2 a $15 - 19$

  b

Reading score	Frequency	Midpoint	fx
0–4	15	2	30
5–9	60	7	420
10–14	125	12	1500
15–19	260	17	4420
20–24	250	22	5500
25–29	200	27	5400
30–34	90	32	2880

    $\frac{20\,150}{1000} = 20.15$

3 44 grams

4 a £100 $\leqslant x <$ £150

  b £150 $\leqslant x <$ £200

  c $\frac{6600}{40} = £165$

  d Probably the median as there are two quite isolated high values, which will make the mean high.

5 a $25\,280 \div 1000 = 25.280\,\text{g}$

  b No, the frequencies immediately show that some packets are underweight.

  c $20 + (733/2) = 386.5$ out of 1000 packets are under the 25 g. This is 38.65%.

  d 38.65% of 3 000 000 = 1 159 500

6 Mean for Machine A = $30.07 \div 100 = 0.3007\,\text{mm}$

Mean for Machine B = $29.07 \div 100 = 0.2907\,\text{mm}$

Mean for machine A is 0.01 mm higher than the mean for Machine B.

The range of the two machines is similar as far as it is possible to tell from grouped data.

Machine A is producing paper much closer to the desired thickness.

7 a 1.105 t

  b The data are grouped so we do not know any of the exact values.

8 a $20 \leqslant t < 30$

  b It is not possible to calculate a midpoint.

  c $50 \leqslant t < 80$ (as a midpoint of 65 has been used by Yasmina)

Assess 6

1 **a** Two very high numbers will make the mean large whereas the middle of the ordered data is only 4.

   Alternative: mean of 4 would be a total of 48 for 12 numbers, 33 and 37 alone much higher than this.

   b Two very low numbers will make mean small whereas the middle of the ordered data is 25.

   c Where data has isolated numbers of completely different size to the majority of the numbers, the median is preferable to the mean.

2 **a** One possible answer: 3 4 4 4 5 and 4 4 4 4 9 with ranges 2 and 5 respectively.

   b One possible answer: 2 3 4 4 5 and 3 3 3 3 6 with medians 4 and 3 respectively.

3 **a** 6
   b 5

   c

Score	Frequency	fx
1	19	19
2	26	52
3	24	72
4	25	100
5	22	110
6	33	198
7	21	147
8	30	240
Total	200	938

$\frac{938}{200} = 4.69$

4 **a** 16   **c** 11   **e** 1

   b 12   **d** 46   **f** $\frac{62}{46} = 1.35$ (2 d.p.)

5 **a** 2

   b 4

   c $\frac{143}{36} = 3.97$ (2 d.p.)

   d Mode is the lowest value, which is probably not helpful. Mean is not one of the data values, which is not helpful. Median is best measure here.

6

Number of people in a household (x)	Number of households (f)	fx
1	9	9 × 1 = 9
2	19	19 × 2 = 38
3	9	9 × 3 = 27
4	8	8 × 4 = 32
5	4	4 × 5 = 20
6	1	1 × 6 = 6
Total	50	132

   a mean = $\frac{132}{50} = 2.64$

   median = 2

   mode = 2

   range = 5

   b Median or mode would be the best average to use as the mean gives a decimal answer and you cannot have 2.64 people.

7 **a** 5–9 years

   b

Number of years' service	Number of teachers (f)	Midpoint (x)	fx
0–4	11	2	2 × 11 = 22
5–9	15	7	7 × 15 = 105
10–14	4	12	12 × 4 = 48
15–19	10	17	17 × 10 = 170
20–24	6	22	22 × 6 = 132
25–29	4	27	27 × 4 = 108
Total	50		585

   $\frac{585}{50} = 11.7$

8 **a**

Height, h (cm)	Frequency	Midpoint (x)	fx
$149.5 \leqslant h < 154.5$	4	152	608
$154.5 \leqslant h < 159.5$	21	157	3297
$159.5 \leqslant h < 164.5$	18	162	2916
$164.5 \leqslant h < 169.5$	7	167	1169
Total	50		7990

   mean = $\frac{7990}{50} = 159.8$

   b John's statement is just about possible but very unlikely. Seven students jumped 164.5 cm or over. John jumped 1 m 65 cm which is 165 cm. For that to be the winning jump, the others must presumably have jumped only 164.5 cm.

(Or for those with athletics knowledge, perhaps there was a tie on 165 but John had fewest fails on 'countback'.)

9

Length, x (minutes)	Frequency	Midpoint	fx
$10 \leqslant x < 20$	7	15	105
$20 \leqslant x < 20$	8	25	200
$30 \leqslant x < 20$	16	35	560
$40 \leqslant x < 20$	6	45	270
$50 \leqslant x < 20$	2	55	110
Total	39		1245

mean for 1900 $= \frac{1245}{39}$

$= 31.923076$

mean for 2008 is 45% higher $= 1.45 \times 31.923076$

$= 46.28846$

$= 46.29$ minutes

10 a

Length, l (cm)	Tally	Total
$5 \leqslant l < 7$	ЖН I	6
$7 \leqslant l < 9$	ЖН II	7
$9 \leqslant l < 11$	ЖН I	6
$11 \leqslant l < 13$	ЖН I	6
$13 \leqslant l < 15$	IIII	4
$15 \leqslant l < 17$	I	1
Total		30

b 9.87 cm (2 d.p.)

c 9.74 cm (2 d.p.)

d because the midpoints were used for each group instead of the exact values

11 Clearly there are many ways to determine why one of the data sets would be the odd one out.

Some of the more likely responses (linked to measures from this section) are:

Set A because it has a mean below 2.3, the other two have a mean above 2.3.

Set B because the other two have a range of 3 but set B has a range of 4.

Set B because the other two have a median that is an integer (A = 2, C = 3) B's is 2.5.

Set C because the other two have a mode of 2 but set C has a mode of 3.

Set C because the other two have an inter-quartile range of 1 but C has an IQR of 3.

12 In games Tom won:

Score	Frequency			
	Tom	Sara	Tom fx	Sara fx
1	9	7	9	7
2	11	10	22	20
3	8	12	24	36
4	8	11	32	44
5	14	8	70	40
6	12	9	72	54
Totals	62	57	229	201

	Mean	Mode	Median	Upper quartile	Lower quartile	Inter-quartile range
Tom	$\frac{229}{62} = 3.69$	5	4	5	2	3
Sara	$\frac{201}{57} = 3.53$	3	3	5	2	3

In games Sara won:

Score	Frequency			
	Tom	Sara	Tom fx	Sara fx
1	11	8	11	8
2	8	7	16	14
3	11	9	33	27
4	7	10	28	40
5	8	8	40	40
6	10	14	60	84
Totals	55	56	188	213

	Mean	Mode	Median	Upper quartile	Lower quartile	Inter-quartile range
Tom	$\frac{188}{55}$ 3.42	1 and 3	3	5	2	3
Sara	$\frac{213}{56}$ 3.80	6	4	6	2	4

The means (and other measures of average) show that consistently the person whose mean is higher seems to win the games more often. The hypothesis is supported by the evidence.

(There are little or no differences between the interquartile ranges – they are there for information – the hypothesis was about the average anyway.)

AQA Examination-style questions

1

Height, h (cm)	Number of students	Midpoint	fx
140 ≤ h ≤ 144	4	142	568
144 ≤ h ≤ 148	5	146	730
148 ≤ h ≤ 152	8	150	1200
152 ≤ h ≤ 156	7	154	1078
156 ≤ h ≤ 160	5	158	790
160 ≤ h ≤ 164	1	162	162

Total = 30   Total = 4528

Estimate of mean $= \frac{4528}{30}$

$= 150.93$ (2 d.p.)

7 Representing data

Practise... 7.1 Stem-and-leaf diagrams

1 a

```
2 | 1
3 | 2  5  8
4 | 2  4  4  5
5 | 4
6 | 0  6
```

Key: 2 | 1 represents 21p

b 66 − 21 = 45p

c 44p

d 44p

e $\frac{8}{11} \times 100 = 72.7272...\%$

2 a

```
0 | 8  9  9
1 | 0  2  3  4  4  7  8  9  9
2 | 0  0  1  2  2  4  5
```

Key: 2 | 4 represents 24 marks

b 25

c 18

d 17

e $\frac{11}{19}$

3 b

```
1 | 26  43  46  49  49  50  53  55  57
2 | 05  06  10  12  26
```

Key: 2 | 26 represents 2 hours 26 min

4

```
 8 | 6
 9 |
10 | 3  6  9  9
11 | 0  3  5  7
12 | 5  6
13 | 0  2
14 | 6
```

Key: 10 | 3 represents 103 minutes

This diagram is far better than the one in question 3 as it spreads the data out over a stem of seven rows rather than two. It is therefore far more informative about the distribution than the first.

5 There is no set answer but make sure the stem-and-leaf has min 23, max 65, median 44, mode of 42 and 55 (and no other) and a key.

6 a 170 or 262

b 262 doesn't but 170 does. 170 would change the median from 215 to 213.

c Mode also unaffected as there are four 209s.

7

	Max	Min	Range	UQ	LQ	IQR	Median
Girls	37	12	25	26	15	9	21
Boys	36	11	25	29	18	11	27

Using the measures found girls have a smaller median, meaning that they complete the exercise quicker on average. The ranges are equal but the interquartile range of the boys is larger than that for the girls, meaning that the boys times are more variable.

8

a

Year 7		Year 11
9 9 9 6 5 4	0	7 8 8 9 9
9 8 8 5 4 1 0	1	1 2 2 2 5 6 7 9
8 8 7	2	0 1

Key: 5 | 1 represents 15 tenths of a second

b Using the diagram alone, it is clear that the Year 7s have the three fastest reaction times and also the three slowest reaction times, so there is very little evidence here one way or the other.

c He should aim to collect a larger sample of data.

Practise... 7.2 Line graphs and frequency polygons

1 a

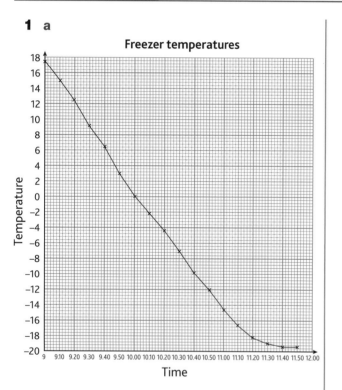

Freezer temperatures

b About −20 as the freezer appears to have reached more or less its intended temperature of operation.

b

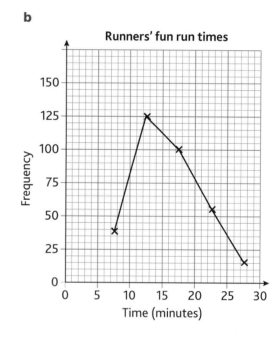

Runners' fun run times

2 a 335

3 a and **b**

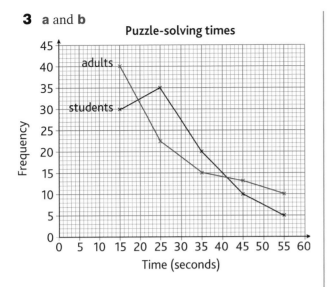

Puzzle-solving times

c The modal group for finishing time was quicker for the adults than the students. The spread of the data (range) is similar for both sets of people.

4 The peak for boys is to the left of the peak for girls indicating that the boys are faster on average. The boys have a plot on 23, which also supports this as the girls do not. The spread of boys' times is greater.

5 a

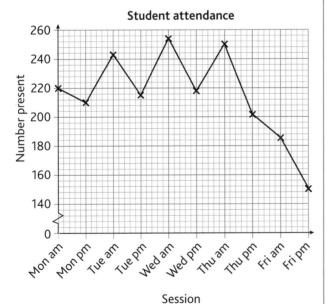

Student attendance

b

Day	Mon	Mon	Tue	Tue	Wed	Wed	Thu	Thu	Fri	Fri
Session	am	pm	am	pm	am	pm	am	pm	am	pm
Percentage	84.61	80.77	93.46	82.69	97.69	83.85	96.54	77.31	71.15	58.46
Percentage to nearest whole number	85	81	93	83	98	84	97	77	71	58

c Both the graph and the percentages seem to show clear evidence of worsening attendance at registration as the week progresses, supporting the principal's thoughts.

6 There are many possible answers to this based on the groupings chosen.

The solution below is based on class intervals each twenty minutes wide, beginning with 1 hour 20 minutes up to (but not including) 1 hour 40 minutes and so on. Remember from Chapter 3 that you should aim for about 4–8 class intervals. The frequency polygon drawn is one example of a frequency diagram – a histogram with equal intervals could equally have been drawn to show the data (see 7.5).

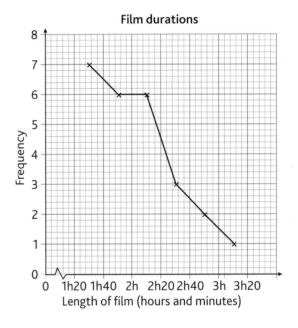

Film durations

Practise... 7.3 Cumulative frequency diagrams

1 a

Height, h (cm)	Frequency	Cumulative frequency
$100 < h \leqslant 120$	5	5
$120 < h \leqslant 140$	12	$5 + 12 = 17$
$140 < h \leqslant 160$	10	$17 + 10 = \mathbf{27}$
$160 < h \leqslant 180$	7	$\mathbf{27 + 7 = 34}$
$180 < h \leqslant 200$	4	$\mathbf{34 + 4 = 38}$

b

Weight, w (kg)	Frequency	Cumulative frequency
$10 < h \leqslant 11$	300	300
$11 < h \leqslant 12$	254	554
$12 < h \leqslant 13$	401	**955**
$13 < h \leqslant 14$	308	**1263**
$14 < h \leqslant 15$	126	**1275**

c

Time, t (seconds)	Frequency	Cumulative frequency
$10 \leqslant t < 30$	43	43
$30 \leqslant t < 50$	65	**108**
$50 \leqslant t < 70$	72	**180**
$70 \leqslant t < 90$	55	**235**

d

Height, h (feet)	Frequency	Cumulative frequency
$100 \leqslant h < 150$	1	**1**
$150 \leqslant h < 200$	15	**16**
$200 \leqslant h < 250$	34	**50**
$250 \leqslant h < 300$	46	**96**
$300 \leqslant h < 350$	16	**112**
$350 \leqslant h < 400$	9	**121**

2 a

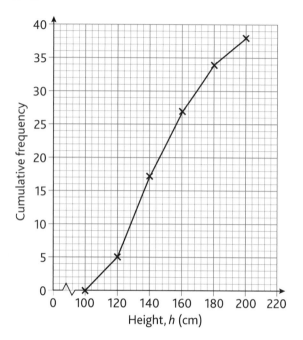

b

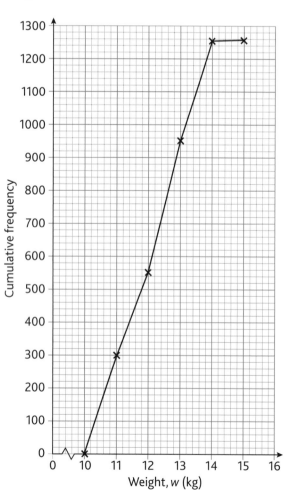

c

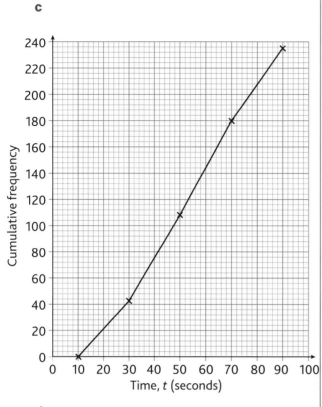

d

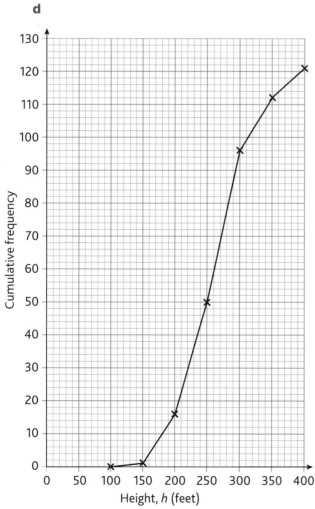

3 a 4.3 ounces

b 3.6 ounces

c 4.85 ounces

d 4.85 − 3.60 = 1.25 ounces

e 2%

f 11%

4 a

Lifetime, l (hours)	Frequency	Cumulative frequency
$50 < l \leqslant 100$	80	80
$100 < l \leqslant 150$	240	320
$150 < l \leqslant 200$	390	710
$200 < l \leqslant 250$	200	910
$250 < l \leqslant 300$	90	1000

b

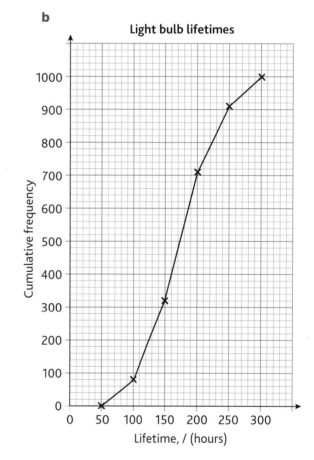

Light bulb lifetimes

c i 172 hours

ii 135 hours

iii 210 hours

iv 210 − 135 = 75 hours

v 7 × 24 = 168 hours in a week

from graph = 460 bulbs below 168 so 1000 − 460 = 540 above

= 54%

d The data is grouped so you do not know any exact values.

5 a

Weight, w (kg)	Frequency	Cumulative frequency
0 < w ⩽ 1	1	1
0 < w ⩽ 2	17	18
2 < w ⩽ 3	72	90
3 < w ⩽ 4	8	98
4 < w ⩽ 5	2	100

b

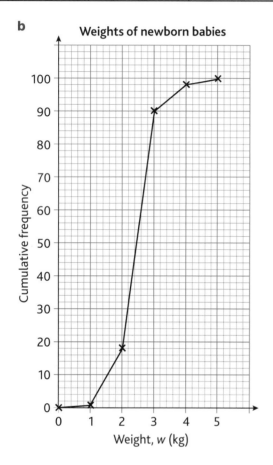

c 2.8 − 2.1 = 0.7 kg

6 a almost certainly 50 mph

b A cumulative frequency graph is needed for the data values in the following table.

Speed, s (mph)	Frequency	Cumulative frequency
55 < w ⩽ 60	27	27
60 < w ⩽ 65	36	63
65 < w ⩽ 72	40	103
72 < w ⩽ 80	11	114
80 < w ⩽ 95	6	120

Upper quartile = 67.5 mph (reading off at cumulative frequency of 80)

The speed limit is therefore higher than the upper quartile and enforcement is not needed.

7 a A cumulative frequency diagram is needed to estimate the median values in the following table.

Hourly pay, p (euro)	Frequency	Cumulative frequency
4 < w ⩽ 5	17	17
5 < w ⩽ 6	56	73
6 < w ⩽ 7	55	128
7 < w ⩽ 8	101	229
8 < w ⩽ 9	39	268

Median is about 7.05 euros (reading off at cumulative frequency of 134)

$\frac{2}{3}$ of 7.05 = 4.7 euros

b Reading off at this value, you can estimate that about 13 of these people are at (or below) minimum wage.

13 out of 268 => $\frac{13}{268} \times 100$ = 4.85%

8 The company has 146 employees and all but six have been with the company for at least 8 years.

The median length of service is 25.6 years. This is an increase of 2.6 years on the figure of 2 years ago, which was 23 years.

The interquartile range is 10% less than 2 years ago when the figure was 14.4* years.

I am pleased to be able to recommend 26 workers for long service awards as they have worked for more than 35 years.

* from graph, IQR is approx. 31.8 − 18.8 = 13 years. If this is 10% less than 2 years ago, then 2 years ago it was $\frac{13}{0.9}$ = 14.444 …

Practise... 7.4 Box plots

1 a 20   **c** 34   **e** 45
   b 29.5   **d** 37   **f** $37 - 29.5 = 7.5$

2 a

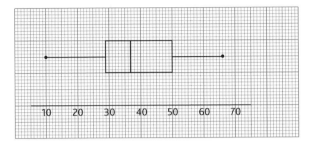

   b As it is the upper quartile, take away the lower quartile, $50 - 29 = 21$

3 a

	Ayton	Beesby
Minimum age	28	2
Maximum age	70	52
Lower quartile age	35	14
Upper quartile	63	43
Median	56	28

   b The population of Ayton is much older on average than Beesby as the median is significantly larger. The spread of ages is similar if based on interquartile range but more spread out in Beesby if based on range. There are no children in Ayton.

4 a

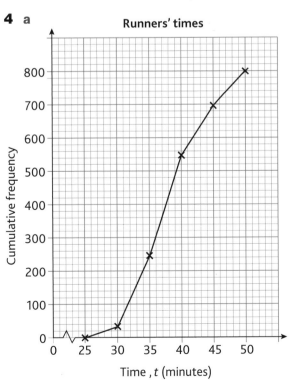

Runners' times

   b For box plot, minimum taken as 25 and maximum as 50. Other measures estimated from cumulative frequency graph.

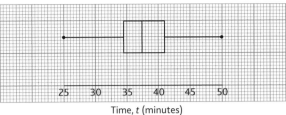

Runners' times

Time, t (minutes)

   c The average time is a little slower as the median is 37.5 minutes compared to 37.1 minutes last year. The times are much less spread out as the interquartile range has come down from 9.9 to about 7.5 minutes.

5 The median waiting time is virtually the same at the main post office as the village post office, meaning average waiting times are similar. The waiting times for the main post office are less spread out than the village post office (inter-quartile ranges of 4 and 6 respectively).

6 a and **ii**
   b and **iii**
   c and **i**

7 Need to obtain box plot for new manager data via a cumulative frequency diagram.

Hourly Sales (£)	Frequency	Cumulative Frequency
£5 up to £10	11	11
£10 up to £15	23	34
£15 up to £20	63	97
£20 up to £25	2	99
£30 up to £35	1	100

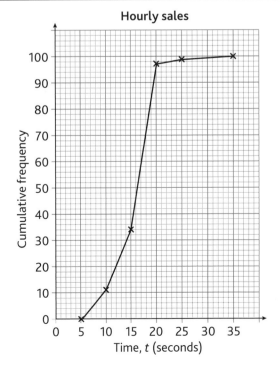

Hourly sales

Time, t (seconds)

Minimum is taken as £5, maximum as £35.

Other measures are estimated from graph above.

Hourly sales

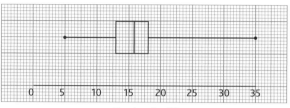

Hourly sales (£)

Under the new manager, average sales are slightly down as can be seen from the slightly reduced median. The spread of sales is also lower as can be seen by the reduction in the interquartile range.

Practise... 7.5 Histograms

1 a

Heights of people auditioning

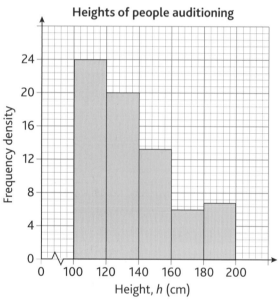

b The final bar would be twice as wide but only half as tall.

2 a

Wages, x (£)	Frequency	Class width	Height = $\dfrac{\text{frequency}}{\text{class width}}$
$100 \leqslant x < 200$	120	100	Height = 120 ÷ 100 = 1.2
$200 \leqslant x < 250$	165	50	Height = 165 ÷ 50 = 3.3
$250 \leqslant x < 300$	182	50	Height = 182 ÷ 50 = 3.64
$300 \leqslant x < 350$	197	50	Height = 197 ÷ 50 = 3.94
$350 \leqslant x < 400$	40	50	Height = 40 ÷ 50 = 0.8
$400 \leqslant x < 600$	6	200	Height = 6 ÷ 200 = 0.03

Wages of factory workers

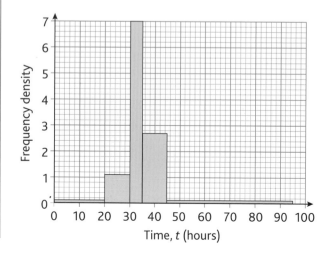

Wages (£)

b 2 or 3

3 a

Time, t (hours)	Frequency	Class Width	Frequency Denisty
$0 < t \leqslant 20$	3	20	0.15
$20 < t \leqslant 30$	11	10	1.1
$30 < t \leqslant 35$	35	5	7
$35 < t \leqslant 45$	27	10	2.7
$45 < t \leqslant 95$	4	50	0.08

b

Speed, s (mph)	Frequency	Class width	Frequency density
$55 < s \leq 60$	25	5	5
$60 < s \leq 65$	35	5	7
$65 < s \leq 72$	42	7	6
$72 < s \leq 80$	12	8	1.5
$80 < s \leq 95$	6	15	0.4

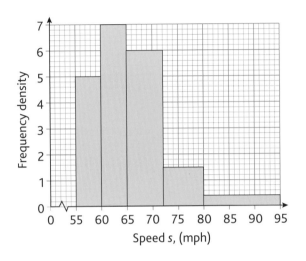

c For part **a**, estimate of median answers between 33.5 and 34 hours.

For part **b** estimate of median = 65 mph.

4

Age	0–10	10–20	20–40	40–60	60–90
Number	4	7	15	11	3

5 a It is unclear where values such as 50 should go.

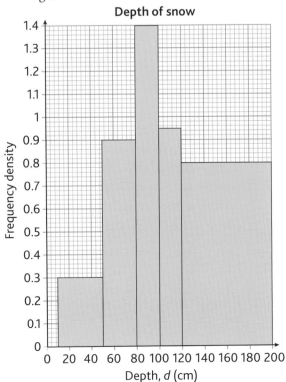

6

Weight, w (g)	Percentage	Class width	Percentage density
$390 < w \leq 400$	10	10	$10 \div 10 = 1$
$400 < w \leq 401$	26	1	$26 \div 1 = 26$
$401 < w \leq 402$	17	1	$17 \div 1 = 17$
$402 < w \leq 405$	33	3	$33 \div 3 = 11$
$405 < w \leq 412$	14	7	$14 \div 7 = 2$

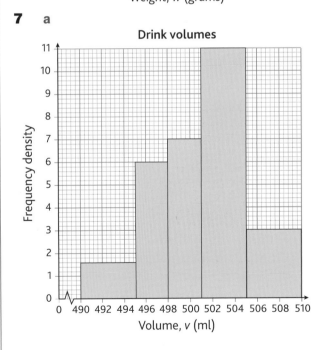

7 a

Drink volumes

b About 38%

c This is a very high proportion under the advertised volume, strictly speaking no drinks should be under the advertised volume for trading standards purposes.

8 a

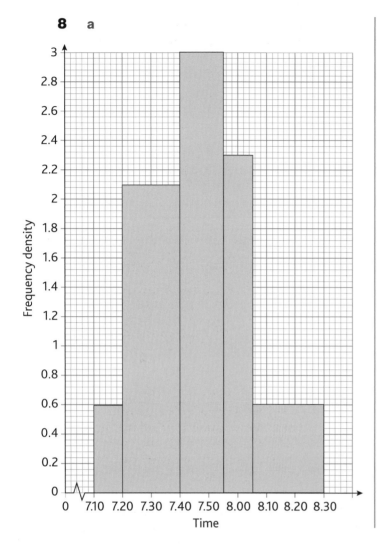

b i This equates to the paper arriving before 7.45 – roughly 50%

ii This equates to the paper arriving before 8.15 – roughly 93%

9 a Variations in the labelling are possible but the boundary values should be as shown.

Weight, w grams	Frequency
$10 \leqslant w < 30$	20
$30 \leqslant w < 40$	42
$40 \leqslant w < 50$	33
$50 \leqslant w < 65$	21
$65 \leqslant w < 90$	5

b 40.91 g (2 d.p.)

Assess 7

1

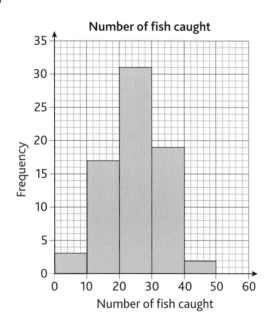

2 a 16 males so median is the mean of the 8th and 9th.

8th height is 174, 9th height is 175, mean of these is

$$\frac{174 + 175}{2} = 174.5 \text{ cm}$$

b Female median height is 167.5

There are only 3 of the 16 males shorter than that height.

$\frac{3}{16} \times 100 = 18.75\%$, which is about 19% as required.

c Female range $= 182 - 149 = 33$ cm

Male range $= 191 - 162 = 29$ cm

The male range is slightly less, showing that male heights are slightly less spread out.

d back to back stem-and-leaf diagram for your class

3 a 13.00 (1pm)

b 10.00 (10am) as it seems unlikely that it would open earlier and there be no people in at all.

c

Time	Number of workers in canteen
10.00	0
11.00	10
12.00	18
13.00	38
14.00	25
15.00	18

d Not really. It is a time series so the structure is appropriate but the context means that the chances of a smooth change between numbers each hour is unlikely. For example, a staff break at 10.30–10.45 would not be shown by this data.

e pictogram or bar chart

4 a 11, 43, 71, 106, 151, 209, 324, 400

b

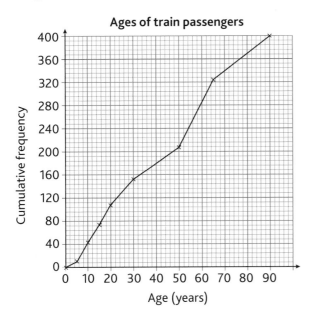

Ages of train passengers

c i 47 years old

ii 19 years old

iii 62 years old

iv 62 − 19 = 43 years

5

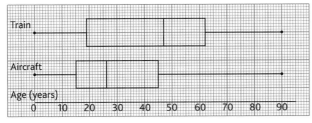

Ages of passengers on train and aircraft

The average age of traveller on the train is much older than on the aircraft as shown by the much larger median.

The range of the two distributions is the same but the interquartile range for the aircraft is smaller than that for trains so the spread of the ages is smaller on the aircraft.

6 a

Ages of train passengers

b Counting squares to half of the area, the median is just under 5/6 through the 30–50 class interval, which gives a median of about 30 + 16.7 = 46.7 years. This is very close to the value 47 obtained from the cumulative frequency graph.

7 a

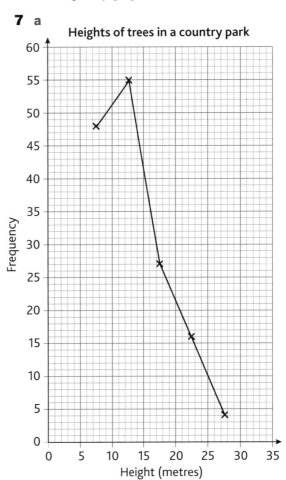

Heights of trees in a country park

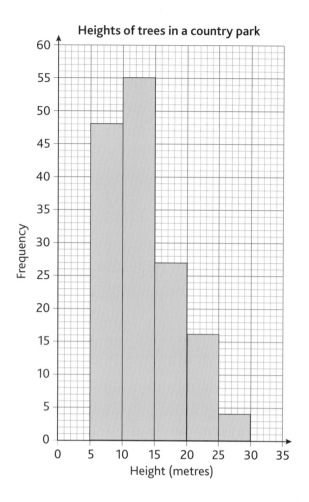

Heights of trees in a country park

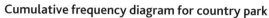

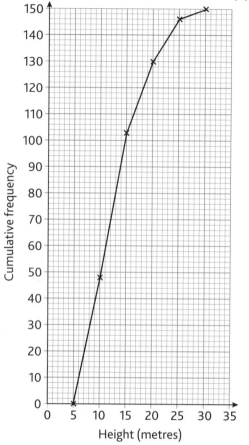

Cumulative frequency diagram for country park

b The midpoint of the last interval is 25, not 22.5.

c

Country park		
Height, h (metres)	Frequency	Cumulative frequency
$5 < h \leqslant 10$	48	48
$10 < h \leqslant 15$	55	103
$15 < h \leqslant 20$	27	130
$20 < h \leqslant 25$	16	146
$25 < h \leqslant 30$	4	150

Local park		
Height, h (metres)	Frequency	Cumulative frequency
$0 < h \leqslant 5$	7	7
$5 < h \leqslant 10$	51	58
$10 < h \leqslant 15$	23	81
$15 < h \leqslant 20$	3	84
$20 < h \leqslant 30$	6	90

Cumulative frequency diagram for local park

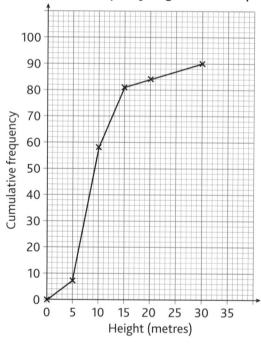

d From the country park graph, estimates are lower quartile = 9 metres, median = 12.5 metres and upper quartile = 17 metres (so interquartile range = 8)

From the local park graph, estimates are lower quartile = 6.5 metres, median = 8.8 metres and upper quartile = 12 metres (so interquartile range = 5.5 metres)

e Local park trees are on average shorter as median is lower. Local park tree heights are less spread out as the interquartile range is smaller than that of the country park.

AQA Examination-style questions

1 a i 40   **ii** 20

  b i 25

     ii

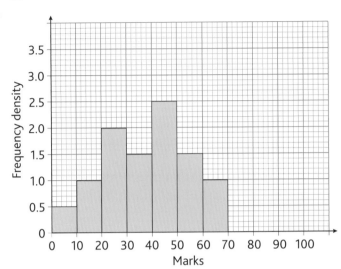

8 Scatter graphs

Practise... 8.1 Interpreting scatter graphs

1 a i positive correlation

   ii negative correlation

   iii positive correlation – probably strong positive correlation

   iv positive correlation

   v negative correlation

  b i The higher the number of hours of sunshine, the higher the income for sales of iced drinks.

   ii The higher the number of cars on the road, the lower the average speed.

   iii The higher the distance travelled, the higher the amount of petrol used.

   iv The higher the number of bedrooms, the higher the price of the house.

   v The higher the number of hours of sunshine, the lower the income for sales of umbrellas.

2 a i strong positive correlation

   ii no correlation

   iii weak positive correlation

   iv no correlation

   v strong negative correlation

  b i The higher the rainfall, the heavier the weight of apples.

   ii There is no correlation.

   iii The higher the number of caps, the higher the cost of the footballer.

   iv There is no correlation.

   v The older the car, the lower the cost.

3 a

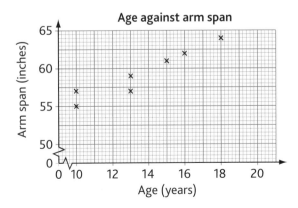

b The scatter graph shows positive correlation.

c The older the person, the bigger the arm span.

4 a

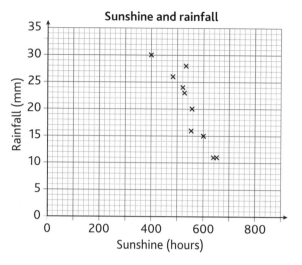

Sunshine and rainfall

b The scatter graph shows strong negative correlation.

c The greater the amount of sunshine, the less the amount of rainfall.

5 a various answers, e.g. age of car against value (strong negative)

b various answers, e.g. age of the car against mileage (strong positive)

c various answers, e.g. age of car against number of passengers (no correlation)

6 a From 0 to 20, the shoe size increases with age, so there is positive correlation.

b Feet stop growing after about 20 years of age.

7 a

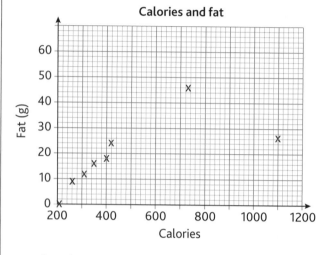

Calories and fat

b There is a strong positive correlation.

c The relation does not hold for milkshakes where there is a high calorie value in terms of fat content. This value is called a rogue value as it does not fit in with the other data.

Practise... 8.2 Lines of best fit

1 a

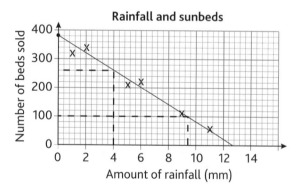

Rainfall and sunbeds

b i 260

ii 9.4

2 a

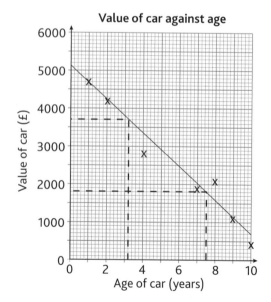

Value of car against age

b i £1800

ii 3.2 years old

3 a

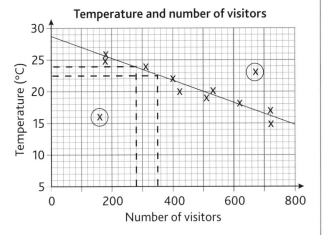

Temperature and number of visitors

b i 280

ii 22.5°C

c Outliers circled on graph.

4 a

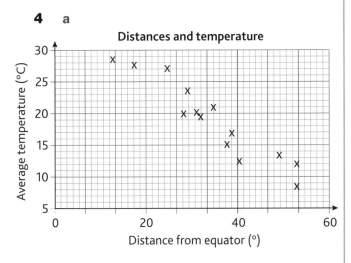

The temperature decreases as the distance from equator increases.

b The average temperature for Dubai is 27°C.

c Other factors affecting temperatures may include time of the year, height above sea level, humidity and so on.

5 a

House price in 2006 (£ thousand)	170	175	190	200	**160**	**185**
House price in 2012 (£ thousand)	225	**235**	**264**	**284**	205	255

b Rashid is not correct. Reading off the line of best fit gives about £245 000.

c £196 000

d £198 000

e These results are both at the edges of the graph so neither result is likely to be more reliable.

6 a

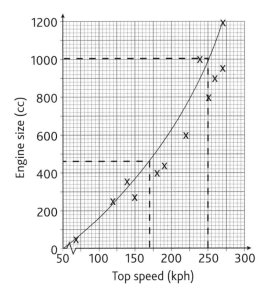

b As engine size increases, top speed also increases showing a positive correlation.

c i 460 cc

ii 1000 cc

d Part i is likely to be a better estimate as the information is in the main body of the graph. Therefore, this result is probably more reliable. Part ii is at the edges of the graph so is probably less reliable.

Assess 8

1

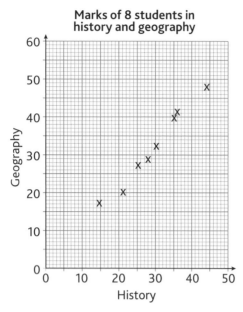

The scatter graph shows strong positive correlation.

2 a

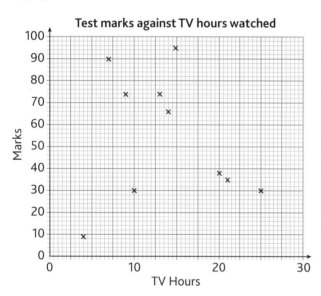

a According to the graph, the more the students watch TV the less they score in the test, which demonstrates a negative correlation between the two sets of data.

b Student '1' and Student '4', do not seem to fit the trend.

They both watched a reasonably low amount of TV but scored low marks.

3 a

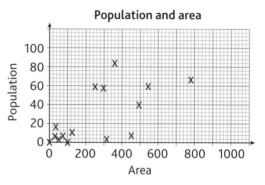

There would seem to be no correlation between the two sets of data.

4 a and **b**

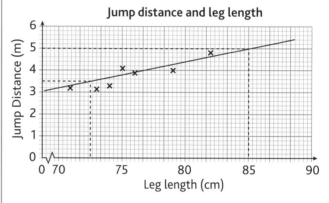

c i 72.5 cm

ii 5 m

d Part **i** is a better estimate as the information is in the main body of the graph.

Part **ii** is at the edges of the graph so is probably less reliable.

5 a 7 metres

b

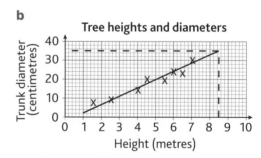

c Strong positive correlation

d i 8.5 m

ii The estimate is beyond the last value marked on the graph so it may not be very reliable.

6 a Number of pages = 140 and weight = 96 g is a rogue value. It is possible that the two figures were interchanged as number of pages = 96 and weight = 140 g is a likely value.

b

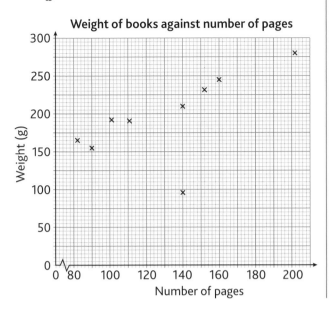

Weight of books against number of pages

Yes, Adnan's hypothesis is correct; the data shows a positive correlation: the more pages, the heavier the book.

AQA Examination-style questions

1 a and **b**

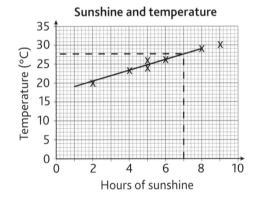

Sunshine and temperature

c 27°C

d strong positive correlation

e Hours of sunshine and temperature were only recorded for 7 days, not the whole month. The rest of June may have had very different weather.

2 a strong positive correlation with an outlier

b i 4 books, 7 kg

ii No effect because all other points already indicate a strong positive correlation.

9 Probability

Practise... 9.1 Mutually exclusive events

1 **b, c** and **d**

2 0.05

3 $\frac{93}{100}$

4 0.999

5 $\frac{7}{10}$

6 a $\frac{5}{15} = \frac{1}{3}$ **c** $\frac{12}{15} = \frac{4}{5}$ **e** $\frac{4}{15}$

   b $\frac{3}{15} = \frac{1}{5}$ **d** $\frac{7}{15}$ **f** $\frac{9}{15} = \frac{3}{5}$

7 a 0.4

   b 0.5

8 0.462

9 One dice as it is a $\frac{1}{6}$ chance of getting a 4 with 1 dice, which is higher than the $\frac{3}{36}$ chance of scoring 4 with two dice.

10 All red shapes are squares.

Practise... 9.2 **Relative frequency**

1 a 120

  b Probably not. 109 is not that far from the expected 120.

2 a 8   **b** approximately 1700

3 a $\frac{9}{40}$ **b** $\frac{21}{40}$ **c** $\frac{1}{4}$

  d The additional 40 draws are unlikely to have the same set of outcomes as the first 40.

4 a i 6   **ii** 22

  b 0.4

5 a 5

  b 0

  c EITHER

    Probably not, after 100 rolls there had been 11 ones compared with an expected 16 or 17.

    OR

    Possibly, as 100 is quite a large sample so the difference between 11 ones seen and the expected 16 or 17 could be significant.

6 a $\frac{56}{270} = \frac{28}{135}$

  b $\frac{84}{270} = \frac{14}{45}$

c $\frac{132}{270} = \frac{22}{45}$

d No, it is $\frac{108}{270} = \frac{2}{5}$

e the 45 for a score of 5

7 a

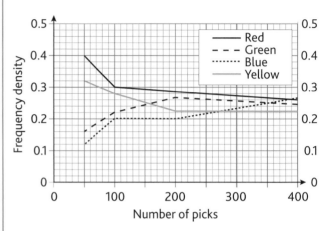

b The relative frequencies after a large number of picks is very similar for the different colours, making it highly likely that there are the same (or a similar) number of each colour in the bag.

Practise... 9.3 **Independent events and tree diagrams**

1 a No, a 3 occurring affects the probability of an odd number (makes it certain).

  b Yes, whatever you pick from the pack cannot affect the outcome for the coin.

2

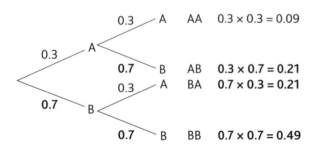

3 0.64

4 a 0.08

  b 0.48

5 a

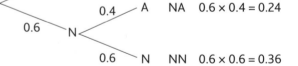

b i 0.16   **ii** 0.36   **iii** 0.48   **iv** 0.64

6 0.176 (3 d.p.)

7 a

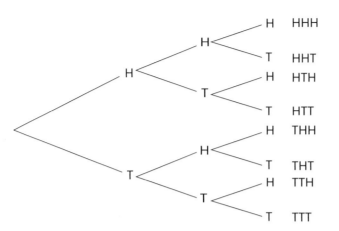

b i $\frac{4}{8}$

   ii $\frac{4}{8}$

8 a

Person 1	Person 2	Outcome	Probability

0.32 S SS $0.32 \times 0.32 = 0.1024$
0.32 S
0.68 N SN $0.32 \times 0.68 = 0.2176$
0.32 S NS $0.68 \times 0.32 = 0.2176$
0.68 N
0.68 N NN $0.68 \times 0.68 = 0.4624$

i 0.1024

ii 0.4352

b They will have had a similar education so are more likely to either speak a foreign language or not.

c 0.904 (3 d.p.)

9 0.42

10 You are multiplying probabilities that cannot be more than 1. Multiply by 1, the result is the same, multiply by a decimal, the result is smaller.

Practise... 9.4 Dependent events and conditional probability

1 a 0   **b** $\frac{1}{5}$ **c** $\frac{1}{5}$ **d** $\frac{4}{5}$ **e** 1

2

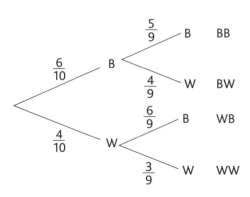

a $\frac{6}{10} \times \frac{5}{9} = \frac{30}{90} = \frac{1}{3}$

b $\frac{4}{10} \times \frac{3}{9} = \frac{12}{90} = \frac{2}{15}$

c $1 - \frac{30}{90} - \frac{12}{90} = \frac{48}{90} = \frac{8}{15}$

3

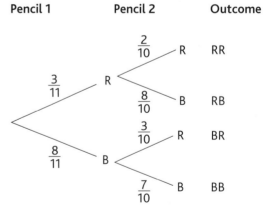

a $\frac{3}{11} \times \frac{2}{10} = \frac{6}{110} = \frac{3}{55}$

b $\frac{8}{11} \times \frac{7}{10} = \frac{56}{110} = \frac{28}{55}$

c $1 - \frac{3}{55} - \frac{28}{55} = \frac{24}{55}$

4 a $\frac{1}{10} \times \frac{1}{2} + \frac{1}{2} \times \frac{1}{10} = \frac{2}{20} = \frac{1}{10}$

b $\frac{1}{10} \times \frac{5}{9} + \frac{1}{2} \times \frac{1}{9} = \frac{10}{90} = \frac{1}{9}$

5 a

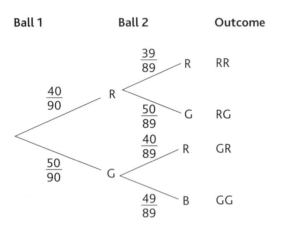

Person 1	Person 2	Outcome	Probability

0.09 S
0.72 → MB SMB $= 0.09 \times 0.72 = 0.0648$
0.28 → N SN $= 0.09 \times 0.28 = 0.0252$

0.91 N
0.26 → MB NMB $= 0.91 \times 0.26 = 0.2366$
0.74 → N NN $= 0.91 \times 0.74 = 0.6734$

b i 0.0648

ii 0.6734

6

Ball 1	Ball 2	Outcome

$\frac{40}{90}$ R

$\frac{39}{89}$ R RR

$\frac{50}{89}$ G RG

$\frac{50}{90}$ G

$\frac{40}{89}$ R GR

$\frac{49}{89}$ B GG

RG OR GR $=> \frac{40}{90} \times \frac{50}{89} + \frac{50}{90} \times \frac{40}{89} = \frac{4000}{8010}$
$= \frac{400}{801}$

7 $\frac{6}{49} \times \frac{5}{48} \times \frac{4}{47} \times \frac{3}{46} \times \frac{2}{45} \times \frac{1}{44} = \frac{1}{13\,983\,816} =$

0.0000000715

8 a i $\frac{85}{200} \times \frac{84}{199} = \frac{7140}{39\,800} = \frac{357}{1990}$

ii $\frac{85}{200} \times \frac{115}{199} + \frac{115}{200} \times \frac{85}{199} = \frac{19\,550}{39\,800} = \frac{391}{796}$

b $\frac{38}{70} \times \frac{37}{69} = \frac{1406}{4830} = \frac{703}{2415}$

9 a $\frac{14}{42} \times \frac{13}{41} = \frac{182}{1722} = \frac{13}{123}$

b $\frac{26}{42} \times \frac{25}{41} = \frac{650}{1722} = \frac{325}{861}$

10 20 socks of which 12 were black

Assess 9

1 a 3 or 4

b around 14 or 15

c around 6050

2 a

	1	2	3	4	5
1	2	3	4	5	6
2	3	4	5	6	7
3	4	5	6	7	8
4	5	6	7	8	9
5	6	7	8	9	10

b i $\frac{3}{25}$ **ii** $\frac{4}{25}$ **iii** $\frac{2}{25}$ **iv** 6

c

	1	2	3	4	5
1	1	2	3	4	5
2	2	4	6	8	10
3	3	6	9	12	15
4	4	8	12	16	20
5	5	10	15	20	25

i $\frac{3}{25}$ **ii** $\frac{2}{25}$ **iii** $\frac{1}{25}$ **iv** 4

3 a $\frac{45}{250}$ **b** $\frac{36}{250}$ **c** $\frac{114}{250}$

d probably, as the frequencies are quite similar after a fairly large number of trials

e all six frequencies around the 1000 mark (probably plus or minus 50) but not all six frequencies of exactly 1000

4 a $\frac{1}{8}$ **b** $\frac{1}{4}$ **c** $\frac{9}{16}$ **d** $\frac{41}{80}$

5 a $0.12 \times 0.12 = 0.0144$

b that successive days were independent

6 a

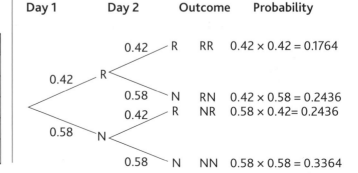

Day 1	Day 2	Outcome	Probability

0.42 R
0.42 → R RR $0.42 \times 0.42 = 0.1764$
0.58 → N RN $0.42 \times 0.58 = 0.2436$

0.58 N
0.42 → R NR $0.58 \times 0.42 = 0.2436$
0.58 → N NN $0.58 \times 0.58 = 0.3364$

b 0.1764

c Weather on consecutive days is often related so the assumption of independence which needs to be made is probably incorrect.

7

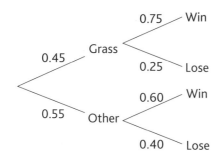

$0.45 \times 0.75 + 0.55 \times 0.60 = 0.6675$

8 $\frac{33}{40} \times \frac{32}{39} = \frac{1056}{1560} = \frac{44}{65}$

9 a

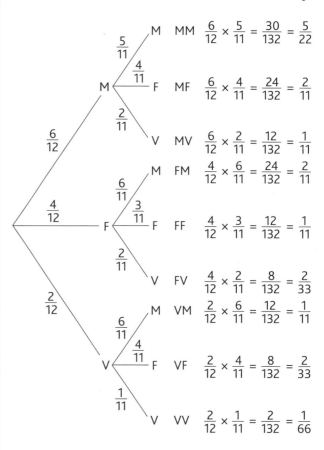

b MF or FM or FV or VF $= \frac{6}{12} \times \frac{4}{11} + \frac{4}{12} \times \frac{6}{11}$

$+ \frac{4}{12} \times \frac{2}{11} + \frac{2}{12} \times \frac{4}{11} = \frac{64}{132} = \frac{16}{33}$

AQA Examination-style questions

1 i 0.2 and 0.5 **ii** 0.1

b 0.9

c 0.18

Consolidation

1 Median   Before 30 mph   After 22 mph
Range   Before 33 mph   After 35 mph

The smaller median indicates that on average the speed is less after putting up the road signs.

The slightly greater range indicates that the speed through the housing estate is slightly more variable after putting up the signs

2 No age ranges given so there will be many different answers given.

No response boxes – unclear whether asking per day/week etc.

A leading question that is trying to gain a particular response.

3 Costlo £152.75 so cheaper than Tescbury even with VAT added on

4 a 3

b No. Nearly all students scored fewer marks on the French test than the German test. So the total would be less than 120.

5 Sugar   406.25 (Allow 410 or 405)
Butter   406.25
Flour   406.25
Eggs   6.5 (Allow 6 or 7)
Vanilla   3.25 (Allow 3)
Milk   6.5 (Allow 6 or 7)

6 **a** £10.59

   b 29

7 **a** $\frac{11}{50}$ or 0.22

   b 52

8 775 metres

9 4%

10 25

11 12

12 Yes, the price is now £279.72

13 **a** 7 or 8

   b (r,b)

Identifies (4,6) (5,5) and (6,4)	Using Option 1
Identifies (1,5), (2.5) … to (6,5)	Using Option 2
$\frac{8}{36}$ ($= \frac{2}{9}$)	Need to see 8/36

   c
Option 1	Option 2
Moves 5	Moves 2
5 to go	8 to go

Identifies outcomes or gives probability for the number of squares left $\frac{4}{36}$ $\frac{10}{36}$

He should choose option 2 because scoring 8 on the next go is more likely than scoring 5.

14 **a** 110.9

   b 567.89

15 **a** 3^0 $0.25^{\frac{1}{2}}$ 1.5 3 10^{-1} 2^{-3}

   b 0.59 cm

16 **a** 9000 or 9×10^3

   b 7.5×10^{-3}

17 Total population = 6.399×10^9

   Total area = 1.3443×10^{11}

$6.399 \times 10^9 \div 1.3443 \times 10^{-1}$

4.76×10^{-2}

18

Number of pets	0	1	2	3	4
Number of students	14	12	1	2	1

19 £44.00

20 10

21 **a** **i** 0.9×10^4

     ii 8.5×10^{-3}

     iii 4×10^7 or 2×10^6

     iv 3.6×10^5 or 4.9×10^{-1}

   b $b + 1 = 2(a + 1)$ or $b = 2a + 1$

   Recognition of relationship between powers of 10 (1,3), (2,5), (3,7), (4,9)

22 **a** £25,881.25

   b **i** 1.06×1.025

     1.0865

     108.65% = 46 176.25

    ii 46 176.25 ÷ 1.0865 = £42 500

23 163.875 metres

24 $\frac{1}{3} \times \frac{2}{3} + \frac{2}{3} \times \frac{1}{3}$ $(= \frac{4}{9})$ Blue and Blue or Red and Red

    $1 - \frac{4}{9}$ $(= \frac{5}{9})$ Blue and Red or Red and Blue

    Different colour

25 **a** Frequency densities 0.8, 2.4, 2.8, 2.2 and 0

   Group widths 5, 5, 15, 15 and 10

   b 54.5 minutes

26 $\frac{13}{27} \times \frac{14}{26} + \frac{20}{46} \times \frac{26}{45} + \frac{26}{67} \times \frac{41}{66}$

   0.751(5 …)

AQA Examination-style questions

1 **a** The quality of service people receive in standard class could be different to first class so it is important to have a representative number of passengers from each class.

   b 32 standard class, 8 first class

   c Age

2 37.5%